The Chosen Lives
of Childfree Men

The Chosen Lives of Childfree Men

PATRICIA LUNNEBORG

BERGIN & GARVEY
Westport, Connecticut • London

HQ
535
.L86
1999

Library of Congress Cataloging-in-Publication Data

Lunneborg, Patricia W.
    The chosen lives of childfree men / Patricia Lunneborg.
        p.   cm.
    Includes bibliographical references and index.
    ISBN 0–89789–598–3 (alk. paper)
        1. Childlessness—United States—Psychological aspects.   2. Men—
    United States—Psychology.   3. Decision making—United States.
    I. Title.
    HQ535.L86   1999
    306.87—dc21   98–44208

British Library Cataloguing in Publication Data is available.

Library of Congress Catalog Card Number: 98–44208
ISBN: 0–89789–598–3

First published in 1999

Bergin & Garvey, 88 Post Road West, Westport, CT 06881
An imprint of Greenwood Publishing Group, Inc.

Printed in the United States of America

The paper used in this book complies with the
Permanent Paper Standard issued by the National
Information Standards Organization (Z39.48–1984).

10 9 8 7 6 5 4 3 2 1

Contents

Preface   ix

Chapter 1   Not to Be a Father?   1

The Missing Data on Men   2
Men Have a Choice   3
The Reasons Exercise   3
Demographics   3
Types of Decision Makers   4
A Model Decision Maker   5
Early Articulators   7
Acquiescers   8
What Lies Ahead?   10

Chapter 2   Personal Development   13

Ted, 40, Musical Instrument Repairman   14
Nigel, 32, Computer Programmer   16
Bill, 36, Sports Medicine Therapist   18
Phil, 55, Geography Teacher   21

Chapter 3   Relationships   25

How Important Are Relationships to Men?   25
Daniel, 32, Piano Teacher   26
Hugh, 55, Freelance Violinist   29
Colin, 50, Computer Center Manager   32

How Egalitarian Are Childfree Men?   34

Chapter 4   Work and Money   **37**

Freedom to Work   37
Frank, 40, Systems Analyst   38
Greg, 37, Deputy Head of a Primary School   40
Arnie, 27, Software Architect   42
How Satisfied Were the Men with Their Jobs?   44
Money Matters   45

Chapter 5   At Home   **47**

Ben, 54, Rural Library Clerk   48
Murray, 44, CAD Designer   50
Gordon, 32, Microsoft Programmer   52

Chapter 6   Avoiding Mistakes   **55**

Denial of Disappointment   56
The Need to Succeed   56
Simon, 44, Guitar Teacher   57
Bob, 53, Utilities Engineer   61
Graham, 32, Pharmaceutical Salesman   63
A Mature Point of View?   65

Chapter 7   Not Liking Kids   **67**

Roger, 55, Sales Manager   67
Walter, 42, Nursing Informatics Lecturer   70
Steve, 37, Airplane Painter   72
Who Initiates the Childless Decision?   74

Chapter 8   Early Retirement   **75**

Dale, 41, Retired Jaguar Mechanic   75
Matthew, 35, Geriatric Nurse   78
Alan, 51, Elementary School Librarian   80

Chapter 9   Avoiding Stress   **85**

Role Strain   85
Michael, 53, Psychology Professor   86
Thomas, 27, Hotel Marketing Director   88

Nathan, 32, Dulcimer Player   91
Doug, 47, Mainframe Computer Operator   94

Chapter 10   Staying the Way We Are   **97**

Jerry, 42, Newspaper Artist   98
Paul, 42, Company Vice-president   99
Kazuo, 33, Mechanical Engineer   102

Chapter 11   Mixed Feelings   **105**

What If? Regrets   105
Legacy Regrets   107
The Family Name   108
Christian Cross Examination   109
Partner Regrets   110

Chapter 12   Men and Overpopulation   **113**

The Missing Motive   113
Population Concern a Secondary Reason   114
Overpopulation a Primary Reason   116
Realism, Not Idealism   119

Chapter 13   The Father Connection   **121**

Mom's Influence   122
Three Types of Fathers   122
Good Fathers   122
Disinterested Fathers   123
Abusive Fathers   125
Dads' and Sons' Decisions   127
A Solution to Disinterest   128

Chapter 14   To Sum Up   **129**

The Childfree Man   129
Paternal Responsibility? No Way   130
No Big Deal Deciding   131
I Would Have Wonderful Kids   132
My Dad Was Indifferent   132
No Hassles Here   132
Control? Nothing to Do with Me   133
Vasectomy? I'll Get Around to It   134

The Future of Voluntary Childlessness   135

Appendix   137

References   139

Index   141

Preface

Men and women are increasingly postponing marriage, opting for singlehood, and divorcing. One in five women is choosing to be childfree. That means more couples are deciding not to have a child.

How many men are choosing to be childfree? What is men's role in couples' decisions? With the advent of contraception, conventionally, women have been the initiators in a couple's decision not to have a child. Is this true today?

There are countless questions to be answered about childfree men. Fertility data, traditionally, have been gathered for women, but not for men and not for couples, creating an information gap when it comes to men.

That's why I wrote this book. Books celebrating the joys as well as the importance of fatherhood are appearing at an unprecedented rate, but where are the books about the path less taken? Here are a few considerations for men contemplating parenthood:

- It is becoming ever more difficult to be a parent today. The newspapers are full of grim statistics on kids and drugs, gangs, crime, schools, poverty, abuse. The responsibilities of rearing children have grown enormously.

- We know from books written about voluntarily childless women that these overwhelming responsibilities are the major reason why one in five women is now opting out of motherhood.

- Our society views having a child, or not, as a woman's choice, but says nothing about it also being a man's choice. That's not fair and it doesn't make much sense. Somebody has got to say it is also a man's choice and educate men to exercise it.

- Fathers today are expected to fulfill two roles: breadwinner and caregiver. Not only must they provide for their children financially, they are expected to share equally in childrearing. Fathers' responsibilities today bear no resemblance to what was expected of their fathers.

• We live in an era of increasing economic uncertainty, making it harder and harder to provide for ourselves, let alone dependent children.

• Overpopulation threatens to lower the quality of life for all on earth.

My project involved interviews with thirty men in the United States and United Kingdom between June and December 1996. I sent each of them an exercise to complete before we met, titled "Reasons Why People Say No To Kids." Much of the hour-long interview was devoted to exploring their motives for not having children. We also discussed overpopulation concerns in the interview as well as how they made their decision, what reactions it got from family, friends, and colleagues, and how it affects their lives.

The Reasons Exercise is in the Appendix You might want to take it before you read the book. This book is about men, but the exercise is equally useful for women, and couples could use their responses as an aid in considering parenthood.

When I had finished transcribing the interviews and looked at the men's major motives as a possible way of organizing the book, motives turned out not to be very helpful. Everyone said they were childfree to preserve either freedom, time, or identity, whereas virtually nobody had made the choice because of motives having to do with control, money, or possibly being disappointed with children had they had them.

So I sorted the interviews according to what seemed each man's major theme. The workaholics stood out, as did the men who wanted time for personal development. The men who primarily were motivated to reduce stress made an obvious group, as did homebodies. And so it went. Nine types of men emerged and chapters 2 through 10 are devoted to these types. Chapters 11 through 13 are devoted to mixed feelings about the decision, overpopulation as a motive, and their fathers' influence upon the decision. Chapter 14 sums up the book.

The Chosen Lives
of Childfree Men

Chapter 1

Not to Be a Father?

Population is stabilising not because we are looking out for posterity, nor for society as a whole, and certainly not for our genes, but because we are looking out for ourselves. The world over people, rich and poor, are trying to juggle different aspects of their lives—work, family, friendships, pleasure—in the pursuit of happiness. For most of us, it now seems that having more than two or three children (indeed, for some of us, having any at all) is to risk letting those juggling balls crash to the floor.

We have a completely different mindset to our ancestors of just half a dozen generations ago. We no longer see children as bringing security in our old age. We know we can choose their number using fairly reliable and cheap contraception. Why incur the expense of a big family? And why, when the time and even the love we can put into parenting is finite, risk spreading those precious commodities too thinly? (Nicholas Schoon, 1998, p.15)

Worldwide, the number of people being added to the global population is falling with each passing year. The United Nations says the highest growth rates are behind us and we'll never see their like again. Closer to home, the U.S. Census Bureau says that in 1995 the rates of childlessness among American women had risen to 27% for those between 30 and 34 years of age, to 20% between 35 and 39 years, and to 18% between 40 and 44 years (Bachu, 1997). The same trend is true for Britain. Monthly, if not weekly, our newspapers tell us—in the US and the UK—that one in five women today does not, and does not intend to, have children. But, what does this mean for men? Nobody's saying.

On the other hand, the burgeoning output of books on voluntarily childless women underscores the pressures they continue to be under from our pronatalist society. They feel goaded to have babies by women's magazines, television talk shows, sitcoms, pregnant celebrities, friends, co-workers, and society in general. They are told by total strangers in supermarkets that they don't know what they're missing. That it's not too late. That they'll regret it for the rest of their lives if they don't experience the joys of motherhood.

What's society's attitude toward voluntarily childless men? What reaction do they get from family and colleagues? Are they pressured in the way women are? Leslie Lafayette, in her 1995 book *Why Don't You Have Kids?*, says men don't talk about it for fear of being branded immature and irresponsible, that society punishes them for the mere thought. In fact, we don't have systematic data on society's attitude any more than we have data on how many men are childless by choice. We are clueless as to how actively men are contributing to the global trend toward stabilizing population growth. And we don't know why they are.

THE MISSING DATA ON MEN

All we know about childless men comes from the very first male fertility study ever done by the U.S. Census Bureau (Bachu, 1996). The survey asked just one question: How many children have you fathered? Two summary statistics are of interest in 1992: 34% of men 18 years of age and over were childless compared to 26% of women in this same age group. Also in 1992, 15% of ever-married men and 14% of ever-married women were childless. These are very basic statistics. We have no idea how much of this is voluntary and involuntary, but the figures suggest that the voluntary rate of childlessness might be, if anything, higher among men.

If it is higher, we're still in the dark about men's motives. Childfree women see mothers' responsibilities as overwhelming. What about childfree men? Is responsibility their big issue? We don't know. Many childfree women are convinced their own mothers made too many sacrifices to raise them. Do childfree men think their fathers gave up too much? The majority of childfree women feel they would not have been good mothers. How about childfree men? Do they doubt they'd have been good fathers? Leslie Lafayette (1995) laments, "It is unfortunate that there is such a dearth of research and information available concerning men and childfree living" (p. 154).

This book is a first inquiry into voluntary childlessness in men. It is an exploratory, not a scientific, inquiry, one aim of which is to spur sociologists to collect methodologically sound data. Until that day, these accounts will have to fill the information gap.

MEN HAVE A CHOICE

Women no longer have to follow age-old traditions when it comes to procreation. Why should men? Why can't a man give serious thought as to whether to ever get a woman pregnant? The problem for men is that they must decide way before the eventuality of a pregnancy.

Voluntary childlessness among men and women is still a minority decision, but the reasons for it are mushrooming. Job insecurity demands long hours at work at the same time that society is crying out for fathers' greater involvement in childrearing. Divorce is claiming close to one in two marriages, and leaving in its wake single parenthood and multiple families to be cared for financially and emotionally. The responsibilities of parenthood are awesome, making it more difficult to raise a child successfully in the face of school problems, peer pressures toward sex, drugs, gangs, and delinquency, and media/marketing targeting of children for an endless supply of consumer goods. Also, we live in an age where overpopulation is a threat to the survival of humankind. Certainly in developed countries it's not seen as a man's right to father as many children as he can.

So, if you or your partner are asking questions such as, "Do I really enjoy children and feel a deep need to raise one?" and "Am I ready to take on the responsibilities of caring for and educating a child?" and "Is raising a child something I really want to do with my life?" then this book has hit you at just the right time.

THE REASONS EXERCISE

Before the thirty interviews featured in this book, I had done twenty others with childfree women, men, and couples. Based on what they told me and the literature on childfree women, I constructed a Reasons Exercise. I was particularly influenced by Jean Veevers's 1980 *Childless by Choice*, and Leslie Lafayette's book because both include some interviews with men. Before we met, the men contributing to this book filled out the exercise, and it was the focus of our taped, hour-long, anonymous interviews.

DEMOGRAPHICS

The men are what is called "a sample of convenience." A minority were recommended by friends of friends. A majority responded to appeals through the American Childless by Choice (CBC) and Zero Population Growth (ZPG), and the British Organisation of Non-Parents (BON). The sixteen American and fourteen British volunteers primarily live on the West Coast of the United States and in the

Southeast of the United Kingdom. I did not seek out men of any particular age or marital status. Twenty-eight are white U.S. or U.K. natives, one is from Iran, and one is from Japan. Twenty-two are married or living with partners, eight are single. They range in age from 27 to 55 years.

Most of the men come from middle-class and working-class families. Half have Protestant backgrounds, the rest come from Catholic, Jewish, or "other" households. They are a highly educated group, "educated" being the most reliable characteristic of childfree people. As to how the 22 wives/partners felt about the decision, nineteen equally strongly rejected the idea of a child, three were ambivalent.

On that all-important question of vasectomy, only a third of the men had had one, the earliest occurring at age 26, the latest at age 44. Most avoided fatherhood by being very conscientious about other forms of contraception. The men's names were changed to ensure anonymity.

TYPES OF DECISION MAKERS

Two types of decision makers, postponers and early articulators, are repeatedly found in childfree women, two-thirds are postponers, one-third are early articulators. Early articulators realize as young as five years of age that they don't want children. The postponing process is supposed to proceed something like this: People get married or start living together and decide to postpone thinking about children for some time period. Then the period passes and they go on postponing indefinitely. At some point they finally discuss the matter and decide. Sometimes sterilization follows. However, many women say they never really made a clear decision. Time just ran out. What would men say? What process do they go through?

It turned out that less than a third of the men I interviewed were postponers, whereas half were early articulators. The rest represent a new type I call "acquiescers." In the US and the UK, the decision to have a child still is seen as a woman's choice. Because of this, many men adopt a neutral attitude: They will have kids if she wants them; if she doesn't, they won't.

About couples achieving consensus, Sharon Houseknecht (1987) has said: "It does seem that the efforts of one spouse to persuade the other to accept a childless lifestyle would be effective and less stressful if the preference evolved after marriage and out of the couple's relationship as opposed to an early, determined announcement before the relationship had been firmly established— before both persons had had an opportunity to experience the benefits of a childless lifestyle" (pp. 384-385).

I'm going to use four interviews conducted prior to this project to illustrate early articulators and acquiescers. But first, I'd like to introduce a postponer and model decider, Graham. Graham's story holds lots of lessons.

A MODEL DECISION MAKER

Graham, pharmaceutical products salesman, is now 32; his wife Janet, a freelance illustrator of greeting cards, is 28. They have been married for two years. They live in Yorkshire, England. Graham's family was upper-middle class. His father, a physician, is married for the second time and raising a teenage son. Here is the process Graham went through. (You'll meet up with him later in Chapter 6.)

Before I met Janet I'd been seeing Martha for a year and it was going nowhere. Just when I was breaking up with her, she told me she'd got pregnant, obviously unplanned, and that we should stay together for the child's sake. I said to her, "Far from persuading me that we should redouble our efforts in this relationship, in fact you're persuading me to do the opposite. If we can't hold the relationship together as two adults, I don't know what bringing a child into that equation is going to do, but my guess is it would be disastrous."

I had no intention of getting back with her and a couple of months later she phoned me up and said that she'd had the pregnancy terminated. Then I met Janet and my first thought was that she'd make a good mother for my children. When I think of that emotion now, it was me thinking she'd make a good companion for me because of her caring qualities. So we got married and we had very typically gone, "Yeah, it would be nice to have a child some day. We seem like nice people and we've got a great relationship, so sure, but not now." Being a professional artist is a major commitment, no different from any other career in management, sales, academe, whatever. If you're going to do it properly, you've got to put time into it and a baby dangling on one hip ain't going to work. So we decided to postpone for five years, which then became a sword of Damocles over our heads.

Then I met an old girlfriend for a drink and heard how her marriage was in trouble and she was having an affair. She had a daughter of two and she said that she regretted having that child, which set me back on my heels. I'd heard, "Well, they're difficult, but I wouldn't give them back," and "Blimey, sometimes they try my patience, but I love them." But I'd never had anyone say, "Christ, it was a mistake."

So I came home and told Janet about my friend. In a couple of days we went to our usual pub, destined to have a normal chat, and somehow we ended up talking about children. Why have we decided on this five-year time scale? And for the first time we asked not, "When are we going to have them?" "How are we going to manage having them?" but "Is this the right thing to do? Are children really for us?"

I told her what my father had said some years before. My mother and father were divorced when I was ten, he'd then married Nell, twenty years younger, and she wanted to have a family, so they produced my little brother when I was sixteen. A few years back my father told me to think very carefully before I had children. I asked him why he was telling me this, and he said, "Well, Nell and I were very much in love. Your brother was very much wanted. We both have very good careers. Money was no problem. We had the infrastructure, friends, support networks, nannies, schools, bells on. But it was still fucking hard." Excuse my French, but that's what he said. I was really surprised at that, coming from my dad.

So I said to Janet, if you've got all he has and it's difficult, how's it going to be if you subtract a few of those things? Probably a lot harder. Dad wasn't saying he regretted it, but he was saying realistically it's a handful, a big investment of everything.

I told her I wasn't particularly bothered about passing on my chunk of the gene pool, or curious about seeing a little me. She admitted that, in fact, she'd never felt maternal, she was never a dolly kind of girl. Also she'd had a lot of responsibility for taking care of her brothers as her father was away, traveling a lot. So there is this commonality, which is very important, in that we realized that we both want the freedom to do what we want. I said I wouldn't want to give up my career to have kids, and I didn't see any reason why she should. Realistically, that's what she'd have to do, make the sacrifice. I wouldn't dedicate any time or resources to it. She remarked on her childless friends who turned forty and felt, "Oh, got to decide now, it's crunch time." They went on to have children and now regret it. So she was wary of that biological clock pressure when she reaches that age, and said she didn't want to be hostage to it.

We talked about the effect children would have on our relationship and at the end of that evening we were pretty sure that neither of us had very strong parenting feelings. That was 18 months ago. We never came back from that position. Then within a short time we moved to a nicer area, got a nicer house, and work was starting to get better for me and for her too. Because of my income, she could try her hand at other kinds of illustration. We could see ourselves climbing a little mountain of improving lifestyle. I've been in financial difficulty before and had to go without, and I don't want to go back to where I'm having to go without, for something I don't really want.

Around that time we were using condoms and had a couple of accidents and she had to take a couple of morning-after pills, which was miserable for her, so that sped up our decision-making process. Last of all, we decided to test how sure we were of our decision by telling our friends we were thinking about not having children. We had a party 3 months after the conversation in the pub and talked with a few close friends and they said, "Who'll look after you when you're old? Won't you miss playing with little red buckets? Oh, you'll change your mind." They asked what if I regretted it and I'd ask back just what am I going to regret? Then they'd get vague. "The experience of children?"

So there were a number of events—the pub conversation, my father's advice, the near-misses, my friend who regretted her child, and the party—it all added up. We also read a newspaper article about falling birth rates, and at the end was a contact number for BON. We contacted them and got some information, things you should think about like, "Am I parent material?"

I'm not one to postpone action once I've made a decision, and neither is Janet. If it had been an equivalent operation, we would have flipped a coin, but it patently is not an equivalent operation for a woman. So I said I'd be vasectomized. It's a minor, minor operation done under local anesthetic, and my general practitioner who is a surgeon, was able to do it in his own surgery. I had my vasectomy this last February just gone—a year from that conversation in the pub.

Graham gives an articulate description of the process of decision making. Here is the way it is talked about by most guys.

EARLY ARTICULATORS

Carlo is 36 and lives on the East Coast of the United States. He's an out-of work maintenance mechanic who has been on disability for 2 years, his chronic fatigue the result of overwork. He grew up in a middle-class Italian, Roman Catholic family and married Joan, a nice Catholic girl who wanted him to know on their second date that she didn't want children. Three years after they got married in 1988, Carlo had a vasectomy. But he made the decision not to have children at age 13.

I planned my life out in my teens. I wanted to buy a house as soon as possible. I knew that once I started working, my job was going to be a major part of my life. I wanted to start early to have financial freedom, so I wouldn't be very old when I owned a house, debt-free.

I never had that need to have children. I feel that's why people should have children. Other than that need, there's no reason. A lot of people don't think about it. They don't realize that having children or not is a lifestyle choice. When I was laid off, I knew people my age who had two, three kids, and were now out of work. I don't know how they survived. Right now we're relying on Joan's income.

When times were good, we bought land, a lot of land, to put Joan's dream house on. But now we've accepted the fact that we're happy where we're at. We have a little starter home, but it's ours. Joan had everything really planned out, too, and I kept telling her that things happen that you can't foresee. Sure enough, I got sick and these plans have changed.

When I was working, I worked 6 days, 7 days a week, plus nights, so that was the life. I've never had a high energy level. I knew I could never stand the stress of taking care of children. Working was hard enough and I wanted to minimize the amount of stress in my life. That's why I bought my house right away. It was a good price, I got a low mortgage. I wanted to make sure I could always pay my bills no matter what. For me the biggest advantage to not having children is financial.

Bart is 45 and lives in a little Oregon town that overlooks the Columbia River with his wife Corey, age 39. This is his third marriage. At heart he is an artist and writer, but he pays the bills making picture frames and doing editing and computer processing for businesses.

My choice for not having children was partly based on the recognition that this is something you have to do as a human being in a big human family. Not everyone has to do it. But some of us have to choose this option. There are simply too many people in the world.

When I was a teenager and hormones were coursing through my body and women seemed a wonderful thing, I watched friends getting married and divorced. Early on it just seemed that having a relationship work was not easy. So one of my goals in life was to make a relationship work well. Reducing it down to the two of us simplifies it. Are we together because I make lots of money? No. Are we together because kids need us? No, we're together because we like being together.

My first divorce was because my wife decided to quit taking the pill without asking me and have a child. Fortunately, I found out about it and quickly had a vasectomy. I was 27. My second wife and I had a very good relationship for 8 years. Then she decided she did want children, and so we separated.

I used to be a production manager for a big business communications firm and it was good money. But the creative area of work was the only one I enjoyed working in. So I do a mixture of things now, and I can exist on about a thousand dollars a month in a nearly middle-class style of living. If I had a child, there would be this whole other budget issue. I was talking on the phone last week to an old friend who has a 2-year-old and I made some comment about, "Gee, I don't really care about being rich." He said, "Oh, yeah, right." And my brain went, click, click, he really does want to be rich, and we're not alike anymore.

Our traveling's very often combined with work. Say Corey has a project in northern California and I'll go along with her and we'll spend the night at a motel and spend the next day looking at wild flowers. Or we add on a day after a country craft show where we sell the beaded jewelry we make. It's easy to tell my partner in employment that I want a Monday off. It isn't a real expensive vacation, but it means a lot to us to be able to do it on the spur of the moment.

ACQUIESCERS

Sid is 29 and drives a truck for a living. He's married to Rose, 33, who is a factory worker. Sid was brought up in a Mormon home, Rose in a Pentecostal home. They live in the mountains in Washington state in a new log cabin up a steep canyon road, and they have four horses and three dogs. They have been married seven years.

My decision happened when we were getting married and she said that she didn't want any children. I thought about it and I could agree, because basically I don't have the patience. See this red hair of mine. I watch these young people with kids and the kids are screaming. And I think, how do parents hold their temper? When we lived in the city, I developed an ulcer, ulcerative colitis, because of the awful traffic. I'd have died if I had kids. We moved here and my job isn't stressful at all. Driving is nothing.

As for my parents, they are very involved in their religion, yet they have told me, if we hadn't had you, we could have done this and that, this and that. Imagine. They're so depressed. I don't have a lot in common with them any more. I went my way, they went their way.

The biggest advantage to us having no kids is money. I only went through high school and with my wage, what I make per hour, the advantage is we can afford to have horses. We have a lot of money in horses, we like to go camping, take the horse trailer up and ride, go up when we want, come back when we want.

I look at my best friend, Bob, who lives in a subdivision. Their life revolves around their kids. And he's not satisfied with their sexual relationship. Because they have the kids, it's practically over with. He has to make an appointment. It's sad. One other scary thing about having kids is if the man and the wife don't get along. If they break up, the man's got to pay all that child support. Another of my friends is getting a divorce. They've been married for 7 years, too, and have a 4-year-old. My friend is going through hell. They tried to stay together because of the kid but they couldn't work things out.

The other thing about money is, how secure is any job? If I got hurt, broke a leg and couldn't work? It just depends on what life's going to bring you. You have to hope for the best and make it work. Even if we both lost our jobs, we'd make it. If we had to go out and live in the forestland, or sell everything and live in our car. It's better than selling everything and living in our car with five kids. But if everything goes all right, when I'm 51, I'll have 30 years with the company. I'll get full retirement.

I got my transfer out of the city because the company needed somebody who could go right then. Other guys a lot senior to me wanted my job, but they all had commitments, kids in school. We could say, "Fine, we're out of here."

Sven's 49 and lives in San Francisco. He's a sailing instructor and has been married 23 years to Anna, 47, who is a lawyer. He says Anna has a very low tolerance for children and things that disrupt her routine.

Anna had a lot of doubts about kids and I was neutral. If I had married someone who really wanted kids, we would have had kids. I like children, although the older I get the less tolerant I am.

I had a lot of privacy growing up as an only child, and I need that—my own time to do my own thing. If I get too fragmented during the day with a lot of phone calls, I don't get anything done. I'm enjoying an in-between period right now, doing house maintenance and working on the boat. We need periods like this where we reorganize our life.

It's helped Anna's career that I don't have a high-stress job. I work when I have to or need to. I am also the houseperson. When Anna gets home, she has an In Basket where I put the stuff she needs to see. She gets out of her work clothes while I make dinner. I do 90% of the meals and everything around the house except the laundry. On weekends, if we're not hiking or sailing, Anna works either at the office or at home.

If we had had kids, I would have given it 150%, spent time with the children, given them first priority. You only have one chance with kids. Maybe it's our society's consumerism that makes you think you can buy a new car and be happy, get a kid and be happy, get a new house and be happy, so you get all this stuff and then you've got to take care of it. I take care of everything we have, our home, our dog, our sailboat. You can't compare buying boats to having kids exactly, but there are always consequences after you get something, especially kids.

Anna puts in long hours, a lot of politics, the legal profession is a rat-race, dog-eat-dog job. I have an easy-going personality and she has a bad temper, so we complement each other there, but it would have been very hard if we'd had kids. Having none is probably why we're still married.

WHAT LIES AHEAD?

We need to answer the question: How does our pronatalist society challenge childfree men? Comments you read over and over in sociological and family issues journals run like this: "Motherhood traditionally has been a major role for women, whereas fatherhood has not been a major role for men." "Because the major responsibility for children is women's, their lives are more affected by children than men's." "Males are less ego-involved in the issue of fertility than females."

If these generalizations are true, then it follows that the stigmatization and censure childfree women endure won't be true for men, at least not to the same extent. Family, colleagues, the media, and society in general won't be trumpeting that fatherhood is a primary role for men.

As far as the decision is concerned, is it as demanding, painful, agonizing, and vital to men as it is to women? Are childfree men as influenced by their parents not to have children as childfree women are? Do they feel their fathers sacrificed too much and got too little in return? Is that why they choose not to have kids? Do childfree men doubt, as do many childfree women, that they'd be good parents? How many of them feel they have family histories not worth repeating? How do men's motives to remain childfree compare with women's? If we profile the typical man who chooses not to have kids, what's he like?

The following chapters are devoted to the nine types of men I encountered, starting out with four for whom personal development was most important. They are followed by men whose motives had to do primarily with maintaining a good partner relationship; focusing on employment and making money; enjoying a quiet, home-centered lifestyle; avoiding mistakes; not liking kids; planning early retirement; avoiding stress; and, finally, staying the way they are—not having to change their personalities to be good fathers.

Chapter 2

Personal Development

> We all yearn to shape our own lives, fashion our own destinies.
> But most of us find ourselves in the same dilemma from our teens
> onward. How do we really want to spend our days? What choices
> should we make? What can we do that will fill our lives with
> meaning and bring us the adventure and rewards we seek? How
> do we know we've chosen the right career and the proper goals?
>
> Every thirty seconds, some new technological company
> produces yet another innovation. Your formal education has a very
> short shelf life.
>
> Thus lifelong learning means far more than formal classroom
> knowledge. In a world in which working with people is essential, it
> also means deepening your understanding of yourself and others.
> (Denis Waitley, 1995, pp. 13-14)

In *Why Don't You Have Kids?*, Leslie Lafayette says that childfree
people, compared to parents, are much more involved *in themselves*.
They spend a lot of time discussing jobs and possible career moves
and analyzing feelings and relationships. They do not have the
convenient out from their own anxieties, faults, and disappointments
that parents have—worrying instead about the issues pertinent to
their kids' lives. "Nonparenting adults have no such convenient
escape and often are forced to deal with their own lives—resulting
often in personal growth and other positives. Have a child and you
won't have to spend any time at all examining your own life" (pp. 80-
81).

This chapter is about a major motive among childfree men—
unhindered by the responsibilities of children—to devote as much

time as possible to personal growth, continuing education, and examining their own lives.

TED, 40, MUSICAL INSTRUMENT REPAIRMAN

Ted has been married for the past five years to Cheryl, 43, who is a yoga instructor. They have lived just outside Portland for the past 7 years. This is Ted's third marriage. In his second, he heroically tried to take care of a woman and her child and failed, which is one of the most traumatic life events a man can experience.

Tell me about your decision.

I had a serious relationship with a woman I met in college, and during the summer after graduation, when I was 21, I went to a doctor for a vasectomy. I had a lot of clarity and passion about the fact that I felt no need to bear children, so he asked me to write a statement out. Then he went on vacation and we left town before he got back. So I didn't have it until I was 26. The idea that I had to have a chip off the old block to call my own was simply never there. Also, if I wanted to be responsible about producing children in an overcrowded world, and I had no wish to, why not let it be me who has none?

My first wife's mother had gone to college for the express purpose of securing a husband to have children with. My wife felt that her mother had wasted her talents, and it wasn't something she wanted to repeat. But the night before the vasectomy she got very emotional in a way I wasn't expecting. We eventually divorced and she now has three children. So it had been clear to me at the age of 21, but it hadn't been clear to her.

Did your second marriage dissolve because of anything
having to do with children?

Yes. She had a 5-year-old child and we couldn't make it financially. My deep-felt experience is that without enough money you really get ground down when there's a child involved. I was working as a laborer trying to support this household of three. Anybody who doesn't have the means to easily take care of themselves and their children is in a terrible situation. My little parenting stint was so brutal.

Cheryl knew from the beginning about the vasectomy and when we met, we, too, weren't brimming over with financial stability. We agree there are too many children in the world who need tending and are going to ask for our help whether we volunteer it or not.

Freedom to travel is very, very important to you. Explain.

I haven't traveled in the past 5 years, but my spiritual inclination is to move whenever it's time to move. If I decided to move to New Mexico tomorrow that would be hard with a child. I have chosen a transformative life. I am also here for Cheryl as she grows. The one performance rating I'm interested in is that she's moving and acting from her heart. Should she choose to leave me, if that's her growth, I want to support it. Her going would be a lot harder, too, with a child. The other thing is that if I'm depressed about something, I can work on it and I don't have to focus attention on a demanding child.

After my second wife walked away I stayed on in our house with my little five dollar an hour job. I didn't say, "Yippee, I'm out of here." I stayed put until she sent me notification that the divorce was finalized. It is very difficult for me to let go of my obligations. The experience of having said I could take on the responsibility of a child and then failing, I got hurt. I couldn't even put food on the table.

You have some real concerns about money. Would you talk about this some?

I don't want any dependents. My mother died when I was 8, and there were five children ranging in age from 9 to newborn. My dad decided not to remarry. He had all the control, he ran the ship. He discouraged us in this highly authoritarian household from having jobs. His reason was, high school isn't a time for jobs, so none of us ever had any money and the lessons you learn about money weren't drummed in. My college expenses were paid by my mother's social security and financial aid. Again, I learned nothing about money. Dad kept us in good clothes. We were sent to parochial schools. Nonetheless, there were gaps in what he taught us, especially how to handle finances.

Does your father know of your decision to be childfree?

No. I wrote him 3 years ago that if we're going to continue as friends, we have to come to account. It's taken me many years to be strong enough and stepped-away enough to say, "This is the way it is, Dad, so if you want to cross the line and be a friend, the first step is coming to terms."

He told me, literally, when I was a sophomore in high school not to try to succeed because the pain would be too much. He told me that success was reserved for people who were destined for high success, and *if I tried, I would fail.* I was an emotional dump for everything that was wrong in his life. He had a low-level clerical job and it wasn't easy. He had to take a lot of crap from whomever was his senior when he was 50 years old and I was at the age where I was starting to feel that people could become whatever they wanted.

It's clear you want lots and lots of time to devote to personal growth.

Yes. My job I accept for being materially in the world, but growing has to do with exploring ideas, educating myself through spiritual texts, engaging in physical practices such as yoga, so that I can be on track where I want to be physically. I really love young children because they remind me of what

I'm striving for. Why can't someone 40 years old with so much more awareness, intelligence, and education have as good a time as a child at play has?

I need time for yoga, meditation, examining ideas from a Sufi perspective, having the possibility of spiritual expansion. I need the capacity to change venues if I find someone who knows more than I do and could offer me something. I'm moving at an intelligent rate, but a teacher can move you that much faster.

You said you hadn't traveled in the past 5 years.

Since college I never lived in one place or kept a job for more than 1 year, that is, until this last stretch here. You can't make all those moves and not pay for it. You walk into an interview and they look through your resumé and think, "When's he going to leave next? There's no history here of a guy who has planted himself." So it's, "Thank you very much. Bye."

I've been able to grow spiritually only with financial stability. If I had a 7-11 job and I'm always thinking about the rent, I can't think about more important things. I want to remember who I came into the world as, and push aside what people want me to be.

The world is getting more and more difficult to live in and I want to be there for whoever needs me. Do you know that management training exercise where they say, "We're on a boat now and we don't have enough food for everybody and somebody's got to go?" The Sufi training I've had would lead me to say, "I'll go." My heart has swelled when I've seen people do similar things. I want to be someone who is ready to do whatever is necessary and do it with a smile. If I were to die tomorrow, I could say to myself, I'm on track for where I want to go. I'm joyous because I'm finally taking care of my life so that I no longer make decisions that can hurt others or hurt myself.

Ted's father was worse than what you've just read. You'll find out why in Chapter 13 where the possibility is floated that being an early articulator is associated with child abuse.

NIGEL, 32, COMPUTER PROGRAMMER

Nigel is single and shares a house in South London with four other men. He was born into a family that was quite poor, of no particular religious beliefs, and he has twin sisters 4 years younger.

Tell me about your decision.

When I was 14, I got very pessimistic about the future of life on this planet. I was also looking at what my parents were going through raising me and my sisters and I thought, "God, I don't want to go through this."

It's been a difficult decision to live with. I find it very hard to find girlfriends. The only women I've met who don't want children, already have boyfriends. I get the impression that almost all women want children. When a baby gets brought into the office, it gets surrounded immediately by women. I went to a dating agency and the issue of children came up and I said I didn't want any. And the woman said, "Well then, I'm sorry but we won't be able to introduce you to anyone."

I hate to admit it, but if I had a girlfriend who wanted children, I might have to go ahead and have them. It would be against my beliefs, definitely, but in a relationship you have to make compromises, otherwise it doesn't work. Children would be a very difficult compromise to make.

*Having time for personal development and education
is most important to you. Why?*

I used to live in a village and I was incredibly bored. Living in London became a great goal of mine. There are so many things to do here, so many possibilities for different courses. I like being able to leave the house whenever I want to, to go to the opera and evening classes. I don't want to have anything that would hold me back from doing these things, not even a pet.

I've taken courses in cooking, massage, learning how to learn, yoga, improvisational dance, physical education in terms of body posture, and politics. I've been involved in several campaigns—human rights, nuclear disarmament, environmental campaigns.

Now that my employment situation has taken over, I have little time for anything else. Fortunately, I'm learning new computer languages in my present job. It's in Dover. I go there Sunday evening and come back Friday. My hours are 8 A.M. to 8 P.M. I've had it for just 7 months. I don't like the travel, but I had to take it.

You really seem glad to be rid of that village.

I am constantly changing my lifestyle. I didn't know how to dance, I didn't know how to cook. Now I spend a lot of time shopping for high-quality ingredients and preparing my own meals. The biggest change is I get up at half past 5 in the morning to do yoga and exercises.

I wanted to buy a flat and was 2 days away from the final contract when I was laid off. This was a year and a half ago. I was unemployed for 12 months. I was very concerned because the technology I was using was out of date. I had great difficulty finding another job and was on the verge of doing a master's degree in computer science when I finally got this job offer.

It's highly likely that I'll have to do that master's degree sometime in the future if I want to keep working. My job is fine only in the short term, but in the long term, jobs are being taken over by programmers in Third World countries, so I'm very unsure about the future.

Back to where I'm living. It's a really disgusting place. When I was made redundant, I had to find somewhere cheap to live, urgently. I put an advert in the local newspaper and this guy phoned up who I knew and he had a place available. It was a big relief. I was claiming benefit and trying to live on £6 a day. I've given up the idea of buying a flat. So you see, my situation is one that precludes raising a child and isn't likely to get any better. I'd

actually feel obliged to give up my job if I had a child because I wouldn't want
to be an absent father who spends 11 minutes a day with my child.

Can you elaborate on that a bit more?

I'd want to be there for them to encourage them to do things like acting,
dancing, swimming, martial arts. I've got very strong ideas about how to
bring up children. The one thing that would really get in the way of those
ideas is a job. It's a dilemma. I couldn't look after a child properly unless I
spent a lot of time with that child, but how could I raise a child with no job?

You've rejected not being attracted to children as a motive?

Mostly I disagree with the notion that you shouldn't have them if you're
not parent material. If I weren't, then children would give me the
opportunity to change. I don't like the idea of not doing something because I
personally have a limitation.

Nigel's reflections on the dilemma of holding a job and being there
for your child may sound naive, but they raise the question of the
workability of choosing to set up a single parent household in an age
when extended families and closeknit city neighborhoods are rare. "It
takes a village to raise a child" is more true today than ever, but
where are the villages?

BILL, 36, SPORTS MEDICINE THERAPIST

Bill has worked as a physical therapist in sports medicine for 7
years. His second marriage is to Diane, 39, a hair stylist. Bill grew up
in an upper-middle class Chicago household; his father was a
businessman, his mother a psychiatrist. While his parents had no
particular religion, Bill has become a Buddhist. He has
undergraduate degrees in Asian Studies and physical therapy. Like
the majority of these men, Bill has not had a vasectomy.

Tell me about the decision.

When I married the first time, it wasn't a practical option. I've been
unemployed and did a number of different jobs before I got a second degree in
physical therapy. I worked as a learning disability coordinator for a major
museum, as a legal assistant, thinking I might go into international law
because I speak Japanese and Chinese, as a rural county cartographer, and
as a massage therapist. With Diane, I told her I wasn't planning on having
any. Her feeling was she didn't know, but she didn't *have* to have them.

Did your relationship with your father influence your decision?

If anything, it would be a factor pushing me towards having children because I have a very close relationship with my mother, and while my father was alive, I had a very close relationship with him. If I were to have children, I would hope we would have the relationships I have had. But there are no guarantees of that. I could hope for that plenty and end up with a child who thought I was the worst person they'd ever met.

Freedom to travel is of primary importance to you. Tell me more.

The trips that I take are very long and fairly risky. I've been once to northern India and twice to Nepal. The treks last 8 weeks in areas where there is a chance that if you become too ill, you won't come home. You are days walking from the nearest radio, so if you don't get better in a hurry, it would be too late by the time someone found you.

It's an area of the world that I'm drawn to and when I want increased inner sanity, I turn toward mountains. It's an area of the world that is still untouched by Western industrial inroads and corruption. Lots of nomads, people who have to live with the land and seasons. I value whatever I can learn from that setting. It's also a part of the world where the population is essentially all Tibetan Buddhist. I've also lived in England and Japan, and I've been in the Soviet Union, the Caribbean, Thailand, Canada, Mexico.

I do a great deal of planning for the kinds of trips I do. The areas I go to are remote even by Nepalese standards, government-restricted regions to foreign travel. It takes about a year and a fair bit of applying for permits and finagling to get in and stay in. Given the risks, children would probably cause me to be less spontaneous about my travels.

Why was having time for personal development and further education important?

I set a high priority on both. They have to do with the furtherance of my personal being, whether that's a spiritual thing or simply gaining further knowledge of nature and my place in nature. I practice Buddhism by formal sitting meditation and I embody it in my daily life in my work with clients, in how I cook, in how I make a cup of tea. For me, that's what Buddhism is, to be totally involved in that moment. Because people entrust me with their health, for me it would be near a crime not to be there in totality.

I maintain that if one truly enjoys eating food, one can tell the difference between a meal that was prepared by someone who was harried and distracted, perhaps by kids, versus a meal that was prepared by someone who was at peace and totally involved in cooking. A Nepalese friend stayed with me for a while and he was amazed that so many people in America eat food that is prepared by angry people. His feeling was, "This is very unhealthy."

I'm not looking to get an MBA or become a doctor, but by law I have to take further education courses to maintain my licenses. That means a weekend course a couple times a year. The bulk of what I mean by further education is personal growth through religious readings. I also want time to practice the Japanese flute.

When people ask me, "What are you trying to get at?" My answer is, "I'm trying to understand the connections between things." The ailments of my patients. My connection with wildlife, or with a tree, or with my wife. A person resonates with a scene in a movie, or a phrase in a song, or with three notes in a passage of music. How do you explain that? Basically, I'm a physical therapist because it allows me to connect with people.

You've never felt a need to have a child?

Not really. I don't need the addition of a child to complete my being. I like life as simple as possible. I feel the need *not* to add another child to the world as a whole. Regardless of how amazing that child might be and how many solutions that child might come up with to any number of problems, it would still be another mouth to feed and there are already a lot of mouths on this planet.

The amount of mystery in the world is decreasing rapidly, and it's directly related to the amount of pavement. They're inversely proportional. People need mystery, and more people equals less mystery and more roads, houses, incursions into the wilderness. I don't think mankind is very good for the world.

In some ways children are the ultimate challenge to the Buddhist idea of nonattachment. The challenge with a child is that your nonattachment doesn't mean rejection. In fact, nonattachment means unconditional love which fits neatly into being a parent. Because regardless of what your children do, you love them. You're not attached to preconceptions about whether you should or should not love a certain thing within them. You're not attached to whether they love you back, dress the right way, get A's, make varsity, or burp at the table. You simply love this being.

There's another issue here. The basic Buddhist tenet is that life begets suffering. Why would you create that? By having a child, you're guaranteeing another being's suffering. No matter what lifestyle you offer them, you're forcing them to suffer. They may reach enlightenment, but you're guaranteeing suffering until they do.

Avoiding stress for you has nothing to do with not having children.

I have a lot of energy and I enjoy kids. One's energy level matches one's enthusiasm for something and if one is truly enthusiastic about kids, one has the energy for them. I'm also a patient person. Patience is very important in raising kids. As far as stress goes, I'm a firm believer that stress is a reaction. It's not an external object; if it were, we could put it out on the curb weekly. People may not think of stress as a conscious choice, but it is. So if children were high up on my list of stressors, it wouldn't be a good idea to have one. But they're not.

The blend of Bill's degrees, his choice of occupation, preferred recreation, and continuing education, is fitting testimony to his declaration, "I don't need the addition of a child to complete my being."

PHIL, 55, GEOGRAPHY TEACHER

Phil is a single, part-time secondary school teacher who lives outside Leeds, England. His family of origin was Catholic and working class. He is one of six children.

Tell me how you came to your decision.

I made the decision when I was 38 as a result of a direct request from my partner at the time. She wanted a child and she wanted me to be the father and said that we should do it within a certain time to fit in with her requirements. Up to that time my thinking about children was underpinned by my background, which was very poor, with a violent and abusive father. I wouldn't wish my impoverished background on anybody. Also I was left-wing, socialist, and had a disregard for paternalistic, conventional, bourgeois family life. I think those two factors operated largely at an unconscious level. At the conscious level I wanted to do interesting work that precluded thinking seriously about children.

When my partner said she needed to have a child, I realized I was more conventional than I'd thought, because she said if our relationship petered out, I didn't need to play a part in raising the child if I didn't want to. But I believe children need a father and a mother and should be the products of a romantic, love relationship. Having a child is a very responsible thing and I feel a child's interests should transcend mine.

The conviction's grown in me that there's something wrong with regarding a child as a mere appendage to your personal development. The child's welfare and future come first. So we fell out over that.

You've said that travel more than anything else has been the main motivator in your life. Tell me more.

I've lived and worked in America, Canada, Australia, Europe. I've had a wonderful life, which I have to keep reminding myself of. So freedom to choose my career and decide what I do and when I do it have been paramount. I was having such a good life, traveling around and earning good money as well as a freelance market researcher, it wasn't until I was put on the spot that I had to decide. Since then my economic circumstances have made children out of the question.

You also want lots of time for further education?

Yes, in addition to my university studies, I've done various personal growth weekend things and been able to grow from someone who was very unaware of what makes up people's personalities to somebody who is pretty aware of what motivates people. It all began a long time ago when I'd been chastened by my first sexual relationship. In the old days, it was part of the culture that the only way a working girl could get a working boy to marry her was to get pregnant. That isn't what happened because by mutual agreement she had an abortion. We were very similar, wanting a choice of careers and lifestyles. After the abortion I tried to settle down in teaching as a regular provincial type, but I realized that the kind of thing that could happen would be to get drunk and get somebody else pregnant and be forced into marriage and finish up having to make the best of it. So I came to London and started to teach in adult education.

I found that being single in London was just the job. No relatives asking when you are going to get married. Wonderful freedom, friends my own age, limitless opportunities, plenty of cash. After a few years I felt I hadn't done as well as I could have at university. I needed to do further academic work, which ruled out having a family. First, I moved into market research where I used my geography background in running surveys. After a number of years of that I was able to support myself freelance and could finish a master's degree in travel and tourism at Strathclyde. Then doors opened abroad in tourism research and off I went.

Today, though, you have some very real employment concerns.

It's always been important to me to be able to change jobs. I was a full-time regular teacher in the 60s and then went back to school and changed careers. Then at the end of the 80s I decided my future should lie back in teaching, which I did in Australia and here. But there have been massive cutbacks, making it very hard for older teachers who are well-qualified and higher up on the salary scale to find work. If there's a regular job available, it goes to somebody who has recently qualified. Economics is the prime decider anywhere in education now.

From that experience when you were 38, obviously wanting to preserve a particular relationhip has had nothing to do with your decision.

Right, the relationship that means the most to me now is with a woman who has grown children, and my continuing decision not to have children has nothing to do with preserving our friendship.

Phil's experience of being asked to father a child but excused from raising it was unique among these men, but his dismayed reaction to women who plan to raise fatherless children was not. All the men I interviewed felt very uneasy about the growing trend toward deliberate, conscious, single-parenthood—adoptions excepted.

It will become apparent as the book progresses that over half of the men were taking courses in one thing or another. They also had a penchant for studying from books, on their own, and from learning by doing. Several were working on car engines from books and one showed me his garage where he had built two wooden kayaks and was now building an airplane from books. So in addition to spiritual and therapeutic "personal development," there was a lot of practical and career-related further education going on. Their wives and partners were even greater courseaholics and completely supported the men spending time growing intellectually and emotionally.

Chapter 3

Relationships

The ideal of togetherness against a hostile world prompted many of the parents of the baby boomers to marry and have children. The ideal of togetherness against a hostile world prompted many of their children to marry, but to avoid having children. Although the childfree gave many different reasons for their choice, most expressed a common theme: They wanted to find happy, fulfilling lives in a private world of love, intimacy, and enjoyable pursuits. (Elaine Tyler May, 1995, p. 208)

HOW IMPORTANT ARE RELATIONSHIPS TO MEN?

Across twenty-nine studies of the voluntarily childless, sociologist Sharon Houseknecht (1987) has found that their second strongest motive was to have a more satisfying marriage. Fifty-seven percent of husbands wanted to preserve their marital relationship compared to 63% of the wives, not that big a difference. I expected relationship reasons to be popular here. After all, the biggest change a couple can anticipate when they have a child is that their relationship will never be the same. Britain's Legal & General Assurance Society (1996) has found that the pressures of looking after children leave only 2 hours a day for partners to be alone together, excluding time spent sleeping. The easiest measurable difference children make in parents' lives is in the reduced time parents have together.

Nonetheless, not many of the men I interviewed gave preserving their partnership as a major motive. They were true to the stereotype that relationships appear more important to women than they are to men. Interestingly, they did talk freely about relationships in other contexts. They valued spontaneously going out to dinner *together*.

They looked forward to early retirement *together*. They enjoyed traveling and vacationing, or staying home and watching TV, *together*. I think relationships are just as important to men. You just have to look for the evidence a little harder.

DANIEL, 32, PIANO TEACHER

Daniel has been married 3 years to Glenda, 32, a primary school teacher. They live west of London. Daniel, the eldest of four brothers, grew up in a middle-class family. His father is a well-known designer for the London stage.

Tell me about your decision and how others have reacted to it.

We've been together for 12 years and early on Glenda spoke about how much she wanted children. I felt the same. I work with children every day and enjoy them a great deal. People have said I'd be a very good father, and if I were to have children, I'm sure I would be. From my wife's point of view, children were too big an experience in life not to have.

Somehow that conviction—that certain things are too good to miss out on—has swung the other way. It now feels that the things that life has to offer, and especially our relationship, are too good to have 25 years of parenting thrust in the midst of it. It was only when I reached my thirtieth birthday that I said, "Hang on a sec, I have to be a grownup now." Glenda was only then finishing her teacher training, and we had no idea what the future held. In 10 years we could still be in a state of change in career terms. We looked at a child from all different angles and decided it was the last thing we wanted.

It's been a firm conviction for 2 years, but no, I haven't had a vasectomy. One never knows absolutely what life's going to bring. What if Glenda died in a car crash and my next partner wanted children? One has to be realistic when dealing with surgical blades.

I haven't told my parents yet. If my mother were to ask, I'd say it's not our thing, but I'd not make a big issue of it. Because my mother talks about how the happiest years of her life were when the children were young. Then there was the experience of our wedding.

Because Glenda comes from a family where there was a nasty ongoing divorce, we decided that the last thing we wanted was to bring the families together. When her brother got married there was this charade of everyone being happy for the day, when in fact they were in court quarreling the rest of the time. We got married at the registry office and I thought my mother wouldn't mind, but in fact she was very upset. She's got a strong traditionalist streak in her and she wanted to wear a funny hat and have church bells ringing. So she might find it galling that her eldest didn't do the proper thing.

My father and I don't talk about personal things, ever. He's a designer and we will go off and see a new stage design together and have a chat about that, but he's never been one for discussing the emotional side of things.

You've indicated you are strongly motivated to keep
your relationship with Glenda the way it is.

Glenda is my best friend. We value our privacy enormously. We are very self-sufficient and time can pass and one of us will say, "We haven't seen anyone for weeks, we better go see someone." I've got a lot of interests that are completely distinct from Glenda's and vice versa. For instance, she's not into cycling so I go off on my own.

We're very close physically, but it's not a clinging relationship. While there's a bottom line of common beliefs we share, it's our differences that bring strength to the relationship. She calls herself a courseaholic, she's always going off to evening classes. She suggested that I go on a music teaching course one summer that sounded hellishly boring, but I gave it a shot. I was feeling down about my teaching and I found it a massive inspiration. I'm now chairman of the organization that runs the summer school. I ceased to feel like a frustrated pianist who wasn't doing enough concerts.

To be close to someone and have the intention to be close until we're 80 years old involves learning to be sympathetic and supportive. The relationship can't exist over a long period if I'm not responsible to Glenda and she's not responsible to me. If I suddenly decide to go off and do something that is totally out of keeping with my character, on a personal whim, it could be quite damaging to her.

Our domestic arrangement is almost 100% me. I'm the cook. I'm very, very fast in the kitchen. The other thing is we don't clean very much, so it's a bit chaotic with things left around in heaps. We love our place because it's near the river Thames and the parks. Our Friday morning ritual is to walk right along the river about three miles and have a pub lunch as a treat.

I also like this house. It's over 200 years old. When I took over this garden, it was just a pile of weeds, and now gardening's become something I really want to do. I'm doing a friend's garden as well. So our home and garden are major things to us.

Is there any other aspect of your relationship that is
important in the context of not having children?

Glenda gets incredibly stressed out by seemingly relatively minor things. That stress is something we can contain, but to bring children into it would be extremely exhausting. She's always trying to do things about it. Like transcendental meditation. It's stressful being a parent at the best of times and if one's got a natural tendency to be high-strung, as Glenda does, then at least 18 years of trauma with a child is something neither of us would enjoy.

Your freedom to come and go as you please also seems very important.

Yes. We both love cinema, theatre, seeing something in the newspaper and saying, "Yeah, let's go." I like going away for the weekend at the drop of a hat without any forward planning. Another aspect to my freedom is that my work at the moment is part-time. Because it's just the two of us, I'm far happier earning much less and having more free time than having to work harder to support someone else.

With Glenda's promotion my plan is to do even less work and spend more time in the garden and on my bike and doing courses. Neither of us has any desire to climb the social ladder or make loads of money. We have close friends who had exactly the same attitude toward life but who also wanted children. Now that the kid has to be supported they're working terribly long hours at jobs they don't like and feeling miserable about it.

With children, when you come back from work in the evening, feeling shattered, your time is not your own. It's the children's time, feeding and putting them to bed. Weekends are running around taking kids to parties and ballet classes. The way it is now, if I'm feeling at a low ebb on a Sunday afternoon and it's drizzling so we're not doing anything, I stick my mountain bike on the car and go to the North Downs and cycle around bridleways for a couple of hours getting covered in mud, which is absolutely wonderful.

What other courses have you done beside the summer teaching course?

I've done a lot of courses as a result of that teaching course, on-going training as a direct result of that summer. Years before that, Glenda got me interested in transcendental meditation when I was doing a lot of local concerts and getting insomnia.

She did an assertiveness training course and I thought, what's the point of that, but I looked at the notes and it was brilliant, so without spending any money, I read her course notes and learned all about it. We spent 2 1/2 years flat out on aikido. That was weekend courses, 4 hours of training every week.

I've signed up for a scuba diving course. I was driving through Chiswick and there was a big poster, scuba diving for £99. Amazing bargain course, 2 days in a swimming pool and 2 days in the sea off of Weymouth. February in Weymouth will be an interesting experience. I did a fixed-wing gliding course as well. I've done an Italian evening class and I'm doing an Hungarian evening class now, once a week.

It seems that your freedom as far as working is concerned seems of utmost importance.

It is. A few years back I decided to become a photographer and I did a photography course and went around taking photographs. I went rapidly broke, but I had a lot of fun out of it.

That's an example of how I suddenly think, I want to change. Glenda was working, I had no responsibility other than to myself financially, so I was able to drop teaching and be a photographer for a bit. I'm happy as a music teacher now, but I very much like the idea of getting professional training in landscape gardening and doing that part-time.

Having time and space for myself is also critical. I spend all day with kids whacking away, so the sound of silence is terribly important to me. I come from a large family, three brothers. It felt even larger because we were in a flat smaller than this, crushed in together, two bunkbeds in a tiny room. In addition, my father loved building things, naturally, and one thing he built was the dream holiday boat for the family to have all their holidays on. The trouble was it was only 19 feet long and he insisted that we sleep on it as a family of six. My holidays up to the age of 13 were with a brother who was not potty-trained on this boat. The crush was exacerbated then, and I have memories of being woken up in the pitch dark because someone had upset the pee bucket.

I can see why you didn't say you weren't attracted to
children but tell me about it anyway.

I work with children, I get on extremely well with children. And it's *not* true that I'm more attracted to adult-centered activities because when I'm with kids, I can easily enter their world. I feel sure I would be a good father from the time that I spend with kids. The youngest children I teach are 5, and with one-to-one teaching you develop a close rapport with kids as an adult they come to trust over several years. They quite open up to you.

Daniel's reluctance to have a vasectomy is puzzling. If *their particular relationship* is all important, how does not being sterilized help that relationship? Or is *his marital relationship per se*, present and future to whomever, more important? Because it doesn't make sense to revel in one's job freedom and pity friends who have lost theirs and yet be ready to give up that precious freedom with a change of wives. Another possibility? It's hard for many men to admit to squeamishness where surgical blades are involved.

HUGH, 55, FREELANCE VIOLINIST

Hugh, the only child of a telephone engineer and a dairy worker, has been married 6 years to his third wife, Clare, a 40-year-old violinist with one of Britain's major symphony orchestras. They live in the north of England.

Tell me about your decision and how others have reacted to it.

When I was 29 I got married for the first time, but we had no meaningful discussions about children beforehand. We took it for granted that we would produce a child, but after 5 years she left. Straight away after the divorce I married my second wife. That marriage turned out to be a real rebound and it became clear quite soon that it wasn't going to work out. Then I got friendly with Clare, who was with the same opera company. We were traveling around together, and we talked about children over a period of time before we lived together or got married, and we concluded that neither of us wanted them.

We've received no pressure from either of our families to produce children. My colleagues accept the situation without being judgmental about it. Someone might say, joking, "Who's going to look after you in your old age?" to which my stock response is, "Why should anybody?" Being the sort of person I am, most people wouldn't confront me anyway. I'd tell them to mind their own business. In an orchestra you don't get this sort of chat across the desk. I can imagine people being stigmatized in an office where you get a cup of coffee at the coffee machine and hear, "Hey, when are you going to do your bit for mankind?"

*Your relationship with Clare played a big part in
your decision. Tell me about it.*

I don't think Clare could enjoy being a parent. She's not maternally inclined and she's been anxious that she might have an early demise ever since I've known her. When she was 6 her mother died of uterine cancer and Clare felt isolated and abandoned. She didn't want to put another child in that situation, because there is the possibility of a genetic link with cancer.

She's also worked hard to get her career and it's not the sort of career that can support looking after children. Making music in a full-time orchestra and being a parent are difficult things to achieve. The orchestra works a 46-week year, a 5-day week on the average. They may be away 3 weeks at a time. They work 40 hours a week, 25 hours playing and 15 hours of nonplaying, like traveling to an engagement. They have to work overtime sometimes. Clare is the principal wage earner in our house. I defer to her working lifestyle and timetable. My life is very spasmodic in contrast. The phone will ring and someone will ask me to be someplace in 2 hours or the phone won't ring for 3 weeks.

Why did you two get married rather than continue to cohabit?

It signifies commitment, it's an act of faith to each other. I fixed it all up. We'd already decided that sometime we'd get married, but Clare didn't want to push me because of my history. So I came in this day and gave her this envelope with an appointment at the registry office and I gave her a ring. She'd always said that if we got married, she'd like to wear a ring with stones in it. We were in town one day and saw this very nice ring in a jewelers and asked if they could make one up in white gold. When they phoned with the quotation, Clare said it was too expensive and canceled the order. I went in a couple of days later and said to make it, here's a deposit, but we won't need it until we get married. Then 18 months later I went in and paid the balance. When I gave her the appointment slip I gave her this little box and said, "Oh, you'll be needing this." She fell apart a bit.

Being able to go out and about whenever you please is also important.

We like to be able to say, "Hey, let's go to the Hyatt tonight for dinner." Or let's go over to Stratford-upon-Avon if we have a weekend free. Or, like last night, let's sit in front of the telly and watch a program we've videoed.

We eat out a lot, we go walking a lot, we enjoy going on holiday a lot. I go to concerts when Clare's playing and she comes to mine whenever I'm playing. She supports me in my sporting activities. I'm a rugby referee and I run marathons. She sews, gardens, plays tennis, swims, runs a bit. We keep in reasonably good shape. For our holidays we go to small Greek islands with not great numbers of people. I have a Greek class Monday nights. Keeps the brain active.

Talk some more about what you do with your time.

Well, we've already covered time for exercise and maintaining physical health. We also want time for further education. I've done an Open University business management diploma, which amounts to half an MBA degree. Arts management is an obvious thing for me to go into. I've applied for two jobs in the orchestra here but I was turned down. People within the organization said, "Oh, your boss'll see you as a threat and you won't get the job." I also considered going in at the bottom of the hotel receptionist chain and working up to hotel manager. Trouble is, we always wait up for each other and if I were coming off a late shift at two in the morning, and she had to get up early to make a 10:30 rehearsal, there's no way she could prepare for her work. Age 55 is the wrong end of the spectrum to change careers, but somebody one day may say, "I could do with a guy like you who's been around a bit."

Clare's doing an Open University psychology degree. She's interested in performance enhancement. All musicians in Britain have a finite shelf life. Ageism rules in so many things and music is no exception. If she goes on beyond 50, well and good, but she wants to leave rather than be pushed.

You've said that as an individual, you can't honestly say you've never felt the need to have children.

That's right. If Clare had wanted children, I might have gone along with the idea. I didn't set out to find someone who didn't want them. We have friends and neighbors who have children with whom we go walking and have meals regularly. Clare likes children, but not for herself. Seventy-five percent of her decision was that her mother died when she was young, and the other 25% has developed over time because of her career, plus she's always said she doesn't have that magical maternal instinct.

What kind of arrangement do you have at home?

We share most chores. I'll have supper ready when she comes in from work. My mother always said if I hadn't gone into music, I'd have gone into cooking. If there's ironing to do, I do it. I've been ironing my dress shirts for years. If we'd gone down the road of having children, it would probably have been me who stayed home and looked after them. It's a joke at the supermarket, because I do the shopping, when Clare goes in the manager asks, "Would you like a map of the store?"

Hugh is a good example of an acquiescer. Clearly, if he was going to marry Clare, he had to accept that they would not have children. Like Daniel, he actually likes spending time with children, but preserving his partnership is paramount.

COLIN, 50, COMPUTER CENTER MANAGER

Colin works for a large university in London. His partner, Marianne, age 48, is assistant head of a secondary school in Guildford, an hour out of London. They've been together since 1987. Colin grew up in London's brawling East End. His family was staunchly working-class and of no religion. An only child, he left school early, at 16, with four scholastic exams passed (English language, literature, French, geography).

Tell me about your decision and how your family has reacted to it.

I don't like wearing powder blue shirts, and children are the same thing. They never appealed to me. The things I like to do have nothing to do with children and families. When I met my partner in 1985, and she'd already had her tubes tied, that cemented it for me.

My parents took no interest in whether I had children or not. And they didn't care about my aspiring side at all. When I was a kid my mum told me the East End was where I was born and where I'd always stay. I was only 8, but I thought, you must be joking. Family life for me as a kid was claustrophobic. We lived in my grandmother's house with lots of uncles and aunts around, all over the place all the time, nagging, like Chinese water torture. As a result, I really like time on my own. When Marianne went to South Africa last summer, I flew to California and drove the coastal roads by myself.

In your first marriage, did you talk about children?

Yeah, we were considering it, but we were always a step behind where we ought to have been financially and socially to have children. Children were a possibility, but then we split up. It was after that that I started to work out whether it was a good or bad idea. Then I met Marianne and she persuaded me.

You place a lot of value in being free to come and go as you please.

I can leave work in the evening and go to the cinema, which I do a lot. We can be at home on a Sunday, reading the paper, and say, "Oh, look at what's on. Let's go." We can call up someone, "Want to go out and do such-and-such?" And go. I often meet people straight after work, we go out for meals, go to concerts and gatherings.

We want to avoid the routines that come with kids. We've got no rules. We're not great housekeepers. I do most of the cooking. It's calming, a therapy of some sort. We really like our house. Marianne went to Massachusetts last week, half-term, for the autumn leaves. All this week we've just sat at home in the evening, talking about her trip. Which means that Saturday we'll be frantically cleaning because we've got friends coming over. We've got a nice, big garden and two cats. We always refer to them as our children. They were Marianne's cats, so when we got together I became their adopted father.

You're not the first childfree man I've spoken to who likes cooking.

When I was in school, roles were all very traditional and the boys did metal work and the girls did cooking. I asked my teacher why it was I couldn't do cooking. I didn't want to hammer on a piece of iron, but cooking? Terrific. There are traditional roles to play when you have children. It's something you slip into and I don't like strict roles.

The other thing I want to be spontaneous about is my job. Two years ago, I wanted to go work for an American magazine called *Rhythm Music*. I get the odd piece of writing published with them, articles and reviews. If something had got off the ground, I could have worked over there for a while.

Tell me about not having to be grown up all the time.

Oh, God, how true that is. I have a great fear about being mature when I see what happens to people when they are. I don't want to run through the street naked, but I want to be able to keep my sense of fun. I like a sense of being out of kilter. If you're always sensible about things, always thinking logically, you never use this chunk of intuition.

When I travel I like places that don't make sense. Like Beijing, a bit of this and a bit of that, but none of it made any sense. When we were in Egypt, we took in the pyramids of Giza in a way that is impossible to describe. It's several miles out of central Cairo, but I said to Marianne, "Why don't we walk there? It's a lovely day." But it was tiring and when we got there we paid our money, and because we were so exhausted, we just collapsed for ages looking at it. The experience came through unfiltered because we didn't have the energy to read and cram all the history into our heads. Afterward we walked over the desert to a little village built on the sand and the villagers came out and talked to us. It's great fun stumbling across things by accident, and what happens is the more times you do it, the more times you can find it.

Tell me more about how you and Marianne spend time together.

Right. We're just two people who share our life together. People should be relaxed in their lives. My parents were always worried about me, that I might get involved with dodgy people. The East End was a rough place to live, a lot of flashpoints in the atmosphere. That kind of worry about children is not what I want at all. But I had a good dad, a fun dad, he used to take me out a lot. When I was 8 I knew the whole of the London underground map, how to get from one place to another. He had a bit of wanderlust and passed it on to me.

I want time for courses that have nothing to do with my job, like I did a self-esteem course for a weekend. It was Marianne's idea, just like the therapy I was in for a year, so the self-esteem course was like a booster. The biggest thing I've worked on were feelings that I wasn't good enough, that people didn't want to know about me. Since then I'm more open with people and I find that people en masse are scared of intimacy. So it's nice to have at least one relationship that is totally intimate.

You have said that you have no money concerns. Why is that?

I know it's in the air for a lot of people. Maybe it's because of the way I've been trained. In the late 60s I got a job as a trainee on the computer system at *The Economist* magazine and I learned all about computers. I took all sorts of courses and learned from that. I have no computing qualifications. It's my experience that got me this job. The network department here does lots of short courses and it's easy to keep up. If I did lose my job, Marianne would have enough money to pay for things until I got another.

Consider Colin's words in light of what Sherri Dalphonse (1997) says about childfree people in the Washington, D.C., area. None of her survey respondents said they chose not to have children for financial reasons. Having more money was not the *reason* they remained childless, it was the *result* of having done so. Chapter 4, "Work and Money," takes up why it was the same for these guys.

HOW EGALITARIAN ARE CHILDFREE MEN?

You couldn't help but notice that Daniel, Hugh, and Colin are the cooks in their households and share other tasks fairly equally with their partners. How typical was this? The answer is, it depended on whether the childless wives worked outside the home and the relative levels of the couple's jobs: When wives were employed outside the home, sharing of household tasks was related to the *levels* of the pair's jobs. If a wife's job consumed more hours than her husband's and she made more money than he, the man did most of the housework. When the husband's job consumed more hours than his partner's and he made more money, things veered toward traditional, the woman doing the bulk of the housework. When the pair's jobs were equal in demandingness and pay, housework got divided fairly equally. The exception to this beautiful correlation is a deputy head of a primary school married to another deputy head of a primary school who says he does only 30% because of how he was raised and his mother's ideas about who should do what in her son's household (Chapter 4).

This is a nice follow-up to the observations by Robert Weiss, a psychiatrist who has studied men in depth: "The division of labor in childless marriages differed from that in marriages with children. Couples without children tended to maintain a division of labor somewhere between the 'everybody does everything' of roommates or cohabitants and the sexual allocation of responsibility of a traditional married pair. The men might be more responsible for the heavy tasks, the wives for domestic arrangements, but there was a great deal of sharing. Especially for marriages in which the wives' earnings were comparable to the husbands" (1990, p. 120).

Chapter 4

Work and Money

Voluntarily childless men are characterized by a high degree of job satisfaction, but not necessarily a high degree of job success, as measured by conventional means. They are more likely to have a varied career history. . . . Should the work cease to be pleasurable, they see themselves as free to change jobs as often as they like, and even to quit work entirely. (Jean Veevers, 1980, p. 83)

FREEDOM TO WORK

The cliché is that being childfree gives women *freedom to work* and men *freedom from work*. But, as you'll find in this chapter, it also gives men *freedom to work*. As many as half of the group of thirty men interviewed are extremely devoted to their careers. There is no mistaking that without the responsibility of raising children, the men worked long, long hours if they chose to, for a variety of reasons—to hold on to their jobs, get promoted, gain wide experience as job security, make lots of money, add to their resumes, earn extra vacation time, retire early, and to become experts. Jobs were the primary thing these childfree men wanted time for, even more important than personal development.

In contrast, for most childfree women, careers take second place to other things in life—home and husband, hobbies and outside interests. The cliché gets turned on its head again. While childfree women have the *freedom to work*, freed from the responsibilities of childcare, it is their *freedom after work* that they relish more.

FRANK, 40, SYSTEMS ANALYST

Frank has a Ph.D. in chemistry and has been married 8 years to Millie, 40, who is a housewife. They live in Manchester, England. Frank had a vasectomy 7 years ago. Born into a working-class, Church of England family, he has one younger brother, single, who teaches music.

Tell me about your decision and how your parents reacted.

I never had any feelings of wanting children for as long as I can remember. It was no divine revelation. It developed within myself as early as 12, and in later school years became a firm belief. When Millie and I met, we had very specific ideas about what we wanted in our lives. Having children was one of the things that I didn't want to do because of the time I wanted for other things, and Millie was of the same mind. I'd never been that serious with any other woman before, so children never came up until then.

My parents have known about it for years, because even as a teenager I declared that I did not envisage having children. It didn't bother my dad one way or the other. My mother took the view that it was up to me. I'm not close to my brother so we've never discussed it and we haven't told Millie's parents because they would be very upset. They would quite like to have grandchildren.

As a 12-year-old, you weren't interested in raising children.
Tell me more.

I feel quite strongly that if you do have kids, you do have to make commitments if you're going to bring them up properly. I've got colleagues with children, and their life is not their own. It's incumbent upon parents to start the education of their children, to bring them up in the right manner, from Day One. It's something you can never get away from, teaching them the difference between right and wrong.

It's a very popular topic in this country at the moment because children are less under control these days. Parents have got their kids for years before they ever set foot in a school, and those earliest years are when the psyche of the child is molded. What a lot of people refuse to take on board is that if you choose to have a child, the responsibility for bringing up that child is yours, and yours alone.

I don't dislike children, but I can only take them in small doses. Millie's sister has got two and we have them to our house for a week or so, and they're good kids, but I'm always glad to give them back.

You and Millie from the word go knew what you wanted to
do with your life. What is important to you?

I don't want to share my emotional resources with children. I work a 12-hour day, a lot of it working far from home, so when I come back I want my time to be with her, and the same thing goes for weekends. My colleagues are in the same position, having to work away from home, and when they get home at weekends, they've got to share their time with the kids and their wives. Their families are far more fraught than ours, because I'm not trying to keep so many balls in the air.

We're interested in walking, plus I run 50 miles a week. I run for a club and I race regularly. I'm a long-distance runner and I usually finish in the top 10%. I ran the Manchester marathon a couple of weeks ago and won a medal. We have albums full of pictures from our trips walking abroad. We've been to Iceland a couple of times and done a lot of backpacking and camping in this country. I've also walked in Germany, Andorra, Austria, and Switzerland.

Tell me how you came to spend so much time walking and running.

I get wound up during the day and running has a therapeutic effect, helps refresh the brain. I run every evening. To be able to run competitively to a reasonable standard is a bonus. When I see the state my parents have got themselves into with their sedentary lifestyle, as a reaction I want to maintain a good standard of health right until old age. The only time my father was ever involved in strenuous physical activity was when he was in the war. He had an attack of angina 18 years ago and has been on medication ever since. He has got old quickly and it has to do with lifestyle, diet, and lack of exercise. I always thought he was a bit of a slob, a bit repulsive if he'd been down the pub and came home drunk. He used to smoke as well.

I was aware that other fathers took an active interest in what subjects their children were taking and they'd offer to help with the homework, but my father never took any interest in what I was doing or what was on the school reports. My mother was the driving force behind both of us going on to higher education. She saw my brother had a talent for music and bought him a piano, and when I smashed up my motorbike, she lent me money to buy an old car so I'd have some means of transport to university. I often say to Millie that although I had two parents, I feel like I grew up in a one-parent family.

You've indicated that the disappointments of others' childrearing had nothing to do with your decision.

These are statements that come from a mature point of view. In terms of other people's children, it's only now that I see the problems my colleagues have. At the time I decided not to have children, these things weren't applicable.

Is there any other motive you want to talk about?

Yes, I've got a quite stressful job. I'm in a profession that is very ageist. I was reading a trade magazine this morning about ageism and it said that within the computing profession, only 8% of people are over 40. I don't see myself maintaining my current profession for more than another 10 years. What I see then, assuming we're financially independent, is downsizing my career. I may go into a different kind of work. Or be self-employed doing contracting work independently.

Within the computing world your skills can become outdated very quickly unless you keep up to speed with current developments. So my job is stimulating from the intellectual side. But I've got no room for anything else.

It's the reason why we have no pets. My job involves working away, and we want to be away on weekends and weeks at a time. If you've got pets, you've got to be around to feed them because pets like to be fed at regular times. It's almost like having children, isn't it?

The men I interviewed had three types of fathers—good, disinterested, and abusive. Frank's was the disinterested type. One can only wonder how a father, eager to hear about what happened in school and his son's plans for the future, might have affected Frank's early feelings about having children of his own.

GREG, 37, DEPUTY HEAD OF A PRIMARY SCHOOL

Greg comes from a middle-class Protestant background and has one younger brother. He has been married 15 years to Judith, 37, deputy head of another primary school. They live near the White Cliffs of Dover.

Tell me about your decision and how others have reacted to it.

Judith and I met during the first week of college and we started living together when we were 19. We made the decision not to have children when we got married. We told my mother long ago but she is a great one still for saying, "Did you know so and so's had another baby?" or "I visited a friend whose daughter's just had a baby," and the implication is that she is disappointed that *she* can't say the same thing.

The sort of reaction I get from colleagues is, "Oh, oh dear." Then I say, "No, no. It's out of choice, my choice. I don't want to have children. I work with them all day long." Then they go on to something else. Sometimes there's the You-don't-know-what-you're-missing reaction, but there is more and more acceptance. There is far more pressure on Judith, whereas people say to me, "Good for you. If that's your decision, it's great that you stick to it."

You've said quite forcefully that you want to be able to
come and go as you please.

There's something inside me that says I don't want to do what people tell me to do. People will say, "Why don't you try this?" and I'll go out of my way to do the opposite. My family are business people. My father was a company director, my brother is in business, my uncles are all company directors. I was never interested in going into business, and got interested in teaching when I was 16 and taught Sunday school. I still like going to college and taking courses. Having no children means I can go out of an evening and do what I want to do, shopping, football, college. Weekends, if I don't want to get up til midday, I don't get up til midday. I'm quite career-oriented and I can stay late and finish projects or attend meetings, which is sometimes taken advantage of. People say, "Oh, it's all right for you, you haven't got children." On the other hand, that extra time has been recognized in terms of promotions. I've changed schools four times since 1980, and each time I've moved jobs, it was because of promotion.

When I entered education, teachers had a great degree of freedom. Now, the curriculum is very much imposed on us. But when I started teaching, the idea that I could do what I wanted, really, really appealed. Plus the holidays.

So you're quite career-oriented. Tell me more about your career.

I do not want to be a head teacher. I want to go sideways. I do quite a lot of teacher training and that's the area I want to go into next. I can see that goal as achievable because even now I've got time to do my school job and also do part-time teacher training in history. I've got a certificate of education for history and geography teaching, and a diploma, which is 20% credit toward a master's degree. We have a new qualification in this country called the National Vocational Qualification and I've done an element of that in personnel management. I recently applied for another job—I didn't get it— but it made me realize that I look pretty good on paper.

You keep pretty busy. How do you spend your spare time
and would you comment on housework, please?

I play badminton twice every week throughout the year, cricket occasionally, and I belong to a sailing club where I have a racing dinghy. I like to go out at least once a week in the summer. It gives me a chance to meet people other than educators. There are a lot of people over 50 in the badminton club and a lot under 30, but only two of us between 30 and 50. Judith and I go to a lot of football and motor racing events and concerts. I'm quite an avid newsgatherer, read a lot of newspapers and magazines, and I'm terrible about buying books.

About housework, I'm afraid to say that the division of labor around here is 30/70. I wash the car, cut the lawn. I will vacuum, I will wash up. That's it. I'm a product of my upbringing, of a traditional, middle-class housewife mother. She sees the male as the one who goes out to work and when he comes home, he has to be looked after. Although she knows that Judith and I work identical hours, she thinks that Judith should do more than I do.

You've said you are also afraid of how your own children
might affect your personality.

I don't want my personality to change in ways I don't want it to. I'm fairly authoritarian. It's an act that I put on when I'm at work. If I had to do that when I got home as well, I'd turn into a very grouchy person. The very fact that I can come home and not have to think about work, it's over and done with and I can be myself, allows me to stay who I am. I even write differently at home.

I take children away on organized parties and they always come back and say, "Oh, he's different from what you think." Because in myself I'm very laid back, easy going, liberal, very tolerant of people, but I have to bury that when I'm at school. If I were a parent, I'd be far too lax on some occasions, and over the top on other occasions. I couldn't stick one way or the other.

Basically, I like children and when I'm at work I have to be very child-oriented to do the best for the children who are in my care. I do call them *my* children, and I take great pride when *my* children perform to the best of their ability, as they did at this opening ceremony for the new nursery. We've got

3-5-year-olds coming to school now. We had a balloon launch and a special assembly for the town counciler who is in charge of education in the local authority, all the school governors, former teachers. The children took it very seriously and I was very pleased with them for putting on a good show, because the school's not in the best area. Although we're in the suburbs, we're in the middle of a council estate and a lot of our children come from quite deprived homes.

How do you feel about not leaving a legacy to your own children?

Well, I'll be leaving my money to various charities. I'm beginning to see my real legacy in kids I taught years ago who come back to talk to me. It's nice to hear that they've passed several scholastic exams or have gone on to do well in university entrance exams. Even the ones who aren't very academic come back to talk. One child who told me the first time I took his class, "I'm not doing what you tell me to do," left school with enough qualifications to go into the Army. It was satisfying to see he decided what he wanted to do and got himself in position to do it. When I first met him, I thought, "At the end of the day, he'll be living off social security."

You might typify Greg as a postponer based on what you know of him so far. But check out Chapter 13, "The Father Connection," where he describes how his dad's job affected the family, and how Greg's observations on his train to school convinced him early on not to follow in his father's footsteps.

ARNIE, 27, SOFTWARE ARCHITECT

Arnie, single, with a degree in computer science, spoke vigorously about his capacity to parent should he have chosen to. Arnie works in the port city of Southampton, England, where he shares a big house with two other young men. He was brought up in Swaziland, went to boarding schools from the age of 7, and now on rare occasions visits his parents who live several hundred miles away.

Tell me how you made your decision. What influenced it?

Where I grew up there were a lot of poor people. When I was about 10, I thought, "Why don't people adopt children? If there are all these children, why do people feel a need to have their own? Why not care for somebody else's?" Finally, when I was 19, I felt, "Why should I have anything to do with it at all?"

I did an international baccalaureate at the United World College of Southern Africa, and we had to do community service. It's very harsh out there. There's no social security. There was a hospital nearby where a lot of handicapped children lived whose parents had left them behind. They weren't bad parents, but if you're a subsistence farmer on very poor land and one of your kids has a wasting disease, what can you do about it? I took these children to the local hotsprings to go swimming and I did vision and hearing testing in a primary school. I also worked in nature reserves where the trees were over 400 years old, really, really beautiful. The local population was so poor, they would go in the forest, clear a patch, and pour paraffin around the bases of the trees and burn them in order to grow marijuana. It takes so much out of the soil they couldn't use it the next year so they'd make another patch and this was slowly eating up this whole lovely area. People have to eat.

How have other people reacted to your decision?

I haven't bothered to tell my parents. I've been in boarding school since the age of 7, so effectively that's when I left home. I never see them except for the occasional holiday and I'm not emotionally close to them.

My colleagues at work are very good about it. A couple of weeks ago somebody mentioned it to somebody else when I walked past. So I stopped and said I'm not anti-children, but if you're going to have children, you should choose to have children, and not do it because it's the norm. People nodded their heads and agreed. Most of the women at work have chosen not to have children.

You've told me your job is of primary importance to you. Elaborate.

I want to be free to change jobs. I'd like to work in Malaysia, and with a family dragging along behind you, the harder it is to do that. For the same reason, I would be very unlikely to ever buy a house. Renting, with a month's notice, I can go somewhere else. In the short term, I like being able to work long hours if I choose to. I go in at 10:00 and leave anywhere from 5:00 in the afternoon until 4:00 in the morning.

I really wanted to study economics. But I couldn't find a company in Britain that uses economists the way that I wanted to function, which was to make long-term investments in Third World countries. The investment must be over a long period of time so not only does the investor get something back, but the people invested in get something. The banks in this country are out to make a quick buck and don't care who they burn, so I ended up in computers.

Even so, your work in computers seems satisfying.

I like it so much I doubt I'll ever fully retire. I'll just work less. So I need to sock away enough money in the bank so I can choose what I do. For instance, if I took a job somewhere else now, I wouldn't accept a pay cut unless I knew that in the long term I'd be a lot better off. My present company's done the typical management thing of breaking their promise about pay raises. I'm normally very trusting of people until they cross me. I've only stayed with them because they have let me gain knowledge over a very wide area. The more experience I have working in different areas, the more choices I have where I can go next. I deliberately find out about a very, very wide spread of things. If you work on one product for 6 years, you'll know everything about it, but you'll have very narrow knowledge. I've worked on 6 products in the last 3 years. I'm called a software architect, which means loosely that I have the big picture.

I want to devote as much time to my career as I can and after it, I like the freedom to do what I want, even if it's sitting in front of the TV watching videos. I like it that friends can phone me up and say there's this, that, and the other going on, so I hop on a train and go off to London for a concert or the cinema. I do a fair bit of travel with my job. I've been to the States four times already this year. On holidays, all I do is laze around because I don't *have* to do anything and because I got the holiday travel stuff out of me during my school years.

You've said that you couldn't possibly be disappointed with children if you had them? Explain.

If you're going to do something, you have to do it right, so if I did have children, I'd do my best to do it right and you can't be disappointed with your best. Parenting involves a lot of time spent with children to find out exactly what they want and to help them get it. My parents did the best for me, they gave me the best education they could possibly afford, so I'm used to not wanting for anything. I'd do the same and make sure my children got absolutely the best of everything. They would be as highly educated as possible and speak several foreign languages. I'd produce well-rounded individuals to the best of my ability.

Where did this sense of responsibility come from?

From living in Swaziland. The Swazi people have a very strong belief in personal responsibility. You're what you make of yourself. It didn't matter how poor the Swazis were, they always tried to get the best education they could, and would stay in the school system until they failed. Whereas in this country, my cousins leave school when they turn 16 simply because they turn 16.

Chapter 12, "Men and Overpopulation," summarizes the men's ideas about the impact of overpopulation on the environment and quality of life around the globe. Arnie, and later Alan, who studied in Taipei, Taiwan, make clear how seeing the impact up close makes young men think twice about becoming a father.

HOW SATISFIED WERE THE MEN WITH THEIR JOBS?

Only three men could be said to be dissatisfied, all because of poor pay and working conditions (i.e., part-time positions or located far from home). Even so, they enjoyed at least some of their work activities. That leaves twenty-seven men who were, or had been, satisfied with their jobs. There were those who, with no children, were free *to make a lot of money* and retire early. There were others who were free *not to make much money*, in return for the pleasure of artistic expression.

How satisfied were they? Very well-pleased were a university nursing lecturer, company vice-president, college professor, software architect, school deputy head, and utilities engineer. They all love their work.

Well-pleased but unhappy with the long hours are a millionaire Microsoft programmer and a Japanese engineer. Well-pleased with no real complaints are the rest, from an airplane painter to hotel sales manager, CAD designer to school librarian, geriatric nurse to salesroom manager.

These men go home to cook a gourmet meal, play with their pets, run 6 miles, work on their cars, dig in the garden, meditate, ride bicycles, take in movies, study Hungarian and Greek. In this age of economic and employment insecurity, they aren't terrified by thoughts of being fired. They even entertain thoughts of quitting if they feel like it or changing to something else if they get bored.

What's most important is that no matter what the drawbacks—low pay, long hours, required travel, office politics, poor promotion prospects, incompetent administrators—their jobs are their choice. They can change if they want. They are free to quit at any time and many have done just that.

MONEY MATTERS

When we left their (childfree) house, my daughter said, "No offense, Mom, but these people are much richer than we are." And I said, "No offense, but if we didn't have you, we would be too." According to the U.S. Department of Agriculture, a child born in 1995 to a family earning more than $56,700 a year costs $11,320 in the first year of life. By the time that child hits 18, the parents will have spent $346,980. A recent article in *Smart Money* magazine added in college expenses and calculated that a child born today to that same middle-class family will cost his parents $450,000. (Sherri Dalphonse, 1997, p. 91)

Surely, I reasoned, if women are questioning the inordinately high price of having a child—children cost up to half of women's lifetime earnings, reports Jane Bartlett—men can't be far behind. Sharon Houseknecht (1987) found that 57% of men gave "monetary advantages" as a reason for not having children versus 42% of women. Wrong here. The men denied money was a motive.

Might it have to do with lack of past family money problems? I went back through the interviews to see what had been said about parental poverty. All in all, only a minority had painful memories of the cost of kids to their fathers. They tended to have fathers who were good providers, so perhaps, as a consequence, saw themselves as equally capable.

Might it have to do with lack of current financial problems? The majority have very good incomes; in fact, three of the Americans interviewed have saved enough to become millionaires. The third possibility is that it's connected with the traditional male role of provider—if a man says he has no kids because of the expense, it implies he's afraid he'd fail as a provider.

Why Don't You Have Kids? puts the average cost per kid until age 17 at $250,000 in the United States. In Britain, a supermarket publication, *What Price A Child?*, says it costs £20,000 to age 5 and by the time she or he has been put through some sort of further education, we're talking £100,000. As we said in Chapter 3, having more money may not be the *reason* these men remained childless, but it is certainly the *result* of having done so.

Part of the uniqueness of the lifestyle of childless couples rests upon the simple fact of their relative affluence. If couples are matched in terms of the husbands' salaries, the childless have many times more resources for optional spending than do their parental counterparts. The magnitude of these differences is considerable. With the exception of the very rich, these factors operate at all class levels to produce substantial discrepancies in the standard of living of parental and of childless couples. (Veevers, 1980, p. 86)

Chapter 5

At Home

The childless as a whole value the freedom that accompanies their nonconformity even if they make little use of it. The stress is upon the *ability* to go out, to take exotic holidays, to move house, to emigrate whilst in reality they tend to live "ordinary," "unexceptional," even "dull" lives and to identify with the reproductively conventional amongst their friends. (Elaine Campbell, 1985, p. 67)

A noteworthy feature of our respondents is that they were ordinary people. Although more advantaged than most of middle America, they could hardly be considered exceptional. . . . From the point of view of ordinary people, it is of little consequence if the brilliant and the famous can be happy without children; it is, however, of considerable consequence if ordinary people can. (Jean Veevers, 1980, p. 160)

I talked with Root Cartwright, head of BON, about how thoughtful and farsighted the men I'd interviewed were. He commented:

The downside of having a job today is that it's difficult not to get sucked up in the work culture, which saps people's energy and time and sense of any self that isn't defined by an occupation. These men want to devote such residual energy as there is, not to the self in the sense of me, me, me, but to the self in the sense of breathing space, recharging the intellectual batteries, having the space and the time to remind yourself that there is more to life than the things that you *have* to do.

These men have been able to anticipate the conflicts for time and energy and the difficulty of taking on too much. They may not be happy with the demands that are currently being made on their time, but they were able to recognize that to load on other inescapable commitments, children, would make their lives unbearable.

Since the 1960s, it has been possible for men to question the self-perpetuating process of doing what's expected of you, generation after generation. Men are freer now to do things they want to do, things that make life more interesting than what they have to do to keep body and soul together. What life used to be like for a hell of a lot of men was: Dad went out and earned the money, mother did the rest. These men had jobs that were shit 10 hours a day, leaving no energy for anything else, but eat your dinner, drink your beer, and then sit in the corner full of resentment.

BEN, 54, RURAL LIBRARY CLERK

Ben is a homebody married 24 years to Heather, a 51-year-old administrative assistant. Ben also is an artist with a bachelor's degree in fine arts. His family was Protestant and middle-class. Heather and Ben live and work on Washington State's Olympic Peninsula. After 4 years of marriage, Ben had a vasectomy.

Tell me about your decision.

We thought maybe we'd have children, but we were, right from the beginning, very close to each other and as the years went by it soon became apparent we didn't feel the need for children. We met working at a science museum in San Francisco and started doing things together because we had the same days off. After only a year, we were married. We discovered this place in 1979 on our vacation, went back, sold our house, quit our jobs and moved up here with no jobs, no place to stay. After 16 years we still don't make as much money as we did at the museum, but we love the water, the mountains, the relaxed atmosphere.

I'd never felt very close to children or excited by them. My sister, who is 3 years older, has always been enthralled with kids, has four of her own, and she and her husband have been foster-parents to thirty-five children over the years. I take after my father. My mother was the disciplinarian and the person who brought up the two of us. My dad was hanging around in the background. Whenever we acted up, he'd immediately lose his patience and my mother would take over. A month ago I taught a class in perception, ninety people in this room, and I was so nervous watching the kids and thinking, "Don't touch those things. Don't break anything."

You've said that you are happy as you are and fulfilled with your wife.

We are very much in love, and it gets better every day. We have very few friends, which is pretty unusual. We spend evenings alone together. We play board games or drive up into the mountains. I have a fully equipped etching, print-making studio with a press at home. A number of years ago I had two galleries in the San Francisco area, one in L.A., and several here that showed my etchings. I haven't been in galleries for a while but I want to get back into that. I have ideas constantly for new works of art, but I don't seem to be getting them onto paper. I suffer from chronic fatigue. My doctor says I'm depressed and I've tried various medications but nothing seems to work. If I were blocked off from any outlet for creativity, I'd be very frustrated, so I play around with Paintbrush on the computer in the evening and create all kinds of images. I like working around the house, building shelves, furniture, cat doors for our two cats whom we spend a lot of time with.

You work with children, obviously, yet you aren't attracted to them?

The responsibility of children every day, day after day, would be overwhelming for me. I was a scoutmaster for a few years. When I got out of the Air Force, the local troop asked me to do a merit badge presentation. Before I knew it, I was assistant scoutmaster. I kept a smile on my face but I never cared for it. Then the scoutmaster left for another part of the country and I was scoutmaster. So when I was accepted for college in San Francisco, it was like, "Whew!"

I don't like what being a parent does to men. A guy we know who worked with us at the science museum came up here to get his Ph.D. They had a baby girl and when they came to visit us with the pile of paraphrenalia, before, it had been the four of us interrelating and talking about different things, and now the baby took all of their attention, even when it was asleep. All they talked about was the child's future and what they could do for her.

I've heard that so many times. Tell me some more about your relationship with Heather.

I don't want it to change. Not that it would fail, but it would change. The two of us would turn our attention away from each other and to the kids. Things were going so beautifully early on, we figured, why disturb it by bringing in another relationship when we don't care for kids a whole lot anyway?

Heather says now that she was much more certain she didn't want them way before I was. I always thought that if I had said something about starting a family, she would have gone along with it, but from what she says now, she was much more adamant earlier that she didn't want kids.

You've said you wouldn't have been disappointed with children if you'd had them. Why is that?

Most people seem happy with their kids. I don't see too much disappointment. We would have done a fairly good job if we had had kids. We knew from the beginning that divorce would never be a possibility, even though Heather has two sisters and both have been divorced. That couldn't have affected our children.

You two are in your fifties. Tell me your plans for retirement.

We'd retire as soon as we could, if we could afford it. We'll probably work up til 65. We've been putting as much money as we can aside each month for retirement. If we both work until then, we're both on the public retirement system, which is pretty good. If I should leave, it would cause financial problems, but if I could get a graphic artist job, or even a drafting trainee-type job, I'd grab it.

With only each other to look out for, Ben and Heather can live in an idyllic rural setting and get by fine money-wise as a clerk and office assistant. They are a good example of how a couple gets set into comfortable routines and enjoying one another's company to the extent that they want nothing to disturb the status quo.

MURRAY, 44, CAD DESIGNER

Murray is a computer aided designer who has a vocational degree in drafting. He comes from a blue-collar family and has been married 14 years to Elizabeth, a 42-year-old international accountant. They live in Seattle. Murray had his vasectomy 2 months before our interview; Elizabeth was getting tired of being on the pill.

Tell me about the decision.

Elizabeth and I didn't sit down one day and ask each other if we were going to have them or not. The decision was made for us in that there was no desire to have them. I think that Elizabeth assumed she would have children. But as she got involved in her accounting work, she didn't want to give time to raising them. She does a lot of interesting traveling in her job. She's gone 6 weeks out of the year, most recently to Singapore, China, and Hong Kong. My guess is, if it had ever come right down to it, I would have said that I didn't want them, because another of my reasons is my sister. When she got out of high school she got religion, married, and popped out five kids immediately. Her life from then on revolved around her church and her family. She's the total opposite of me.

So you're another couple happy to remain just as you are.

Yes. We value the freedom to do what we want and not worry about money. We can change our lifestyle, our jobs, go anywhere we want. We go out to dinner three or four times a week. We go on long drives and stay at nice bed and breakfast resorts. We take our RV out a couple times a month. Last time we went up to Campbell River on Vancouver Island and stayed in an adult-only RV park. The people were like us, retired, a little bit older. The men talk about their trucks, the women talk about how they fixed up the trailer and their crafts.

I'm really into cars. There must be at least thirty car magazines here in the living room. I read them every night. I'm restoring a hot rod and I'm spending every night on it because I need to get it done for the summer. I have no qualms on a Saturday morning driving down to Portland for parts. No big deal. Elizabeth will go to her watercolor or tole painting or stitchery class.

You've said you really want to avoid the kinds of routines that children impose.

I don't want to be stereotyped, never wanted to be the 2.1 kids, the mini-van, going to Costco and McDonalds, the American family thing that everybody is supposed to do. You grow up, you go to school, you have a wife, you have children, and then you retire, with grandchildren. I made the conscious choice not to fall into that stereotype and I feel good about that.

My mom's actually proud of me for doing it. I told her 10 years ago that we wouldn't have children, that they were something we didn't need. She said that it was a lot of work and it doesn't always work out. My mom wasn't crazy about my sister having five.

You've also said that you aren't attracted to children. What do you mean?

I wouldn't give children the attention that they need. I see too much effort being made by other people and not a lot of happiness along with it. I wouldn't have been a very good parent and Elizabeth was concerned, too, about how good she'd be. She has a brother who turned out on the bad side, still lives at home, in his forties, doesn't have a great job, was a drug and alcohol abuser in trouble with the law. In her childhood, she had a father who just sat back and watched and a mother who was crying all the time.

She must have suspected, even though we didn't talk about it, that to bring a child in here, it would be her responsibility. I'm not going to change diapers. Don't get me wrong. We're not Ozzie and Harriet. I vacuum and dust and fix everything, take care of the yard. I cook most of the time. We do all our activity-planning 50-50. I've been called selfish for not having children. And I tell people *I am selfish* because it's my life and I don't want to share that much commitment and time that you need to to raise a family. It's hard enough for both of us working 50 hours a week.

You've got a well-behaved dog. Apparently he isn't too much for you.

I feel as responsible toward him as somebody else would toward a child. He gets the best of everything. When we go away in our RV, he goes along. He's got the back of the truck. It's all carpeted for him. He's 4 years old, but we've only had him for a year. He came from an abusive family. We got him from pure-bred rescue through an adoption-type system. We went to a dog show one day and the rescue had brought him to show people. He just clung to us and we to him. When we got him he didn't know how to play, and when you tried to pet him, he would cower down on the floor. He's undergone a complete turnaround. He sleeps next to us at the bottom of the bed, every night.

You've indicated that you've got no particular employment concerns.

I'm not a big career person. I'm not big on climbing the corporate ladder or going back to school and becoming an engineer. Or working overtime, moving to another state, or bringing work home. I want to retire at 55 so we've invested wisely, we're making our money work. We've got stock investments, mutual funds, company 401(k)s, savings. We haven't bought a big house with big payments. I don't think a $2,000 house payment is a wise thing to do unless you're making a triple-figure income. When we retire we're going to travel all over the States. Alaska I'm really looking forward to.

I like my job. I've been with them 5 years. There is virtually no stress because I don't allow it to happen. A lot of people there take it way too seriously.

You're saying your job could be stressful?

Yeah, but I don't get wrapped up in my work like the other guys. I figure, I could take all the stress in and try to do a fantastic job, but what am I going to get for it? I'd get the same paycheck every week.

My big workplace issue, because I don't have kids, is sick leave. If you have children, you can take as much time as you want. If you don't, there's no excuse not to be there unless you're deathly ill. People leave early if their kid has soccer practice or a piano lesson. There have been times when my dog was sick and I've said, "Gotta go. A family member's sick," and I disappear before they ask me which one.

My last question is, was your decision connected in any way with your relationship with your father?

Could be. I had an in-the-background dad. He was a typical blue-collar guy. He'd come home, read the paper, eat his dinner, watch TV. There was no affection there. Having kids probably didn't mean a whole lot to him. Maybe that is why I never had the drive to. The whole neighborhood was like that in the ratpack I ran around with. There wasn't a single *Leave It To Beaver* family, where it's a happy group that does things together all the time. I was never around that.

It's hard not to notice the role that pets play in maintaining a warm, comfortable home and how many of the dogs and cats in this book were rescued. Jean Veevers (1980) claims it is a myth that childless people's pets serve as surrogate children. I think that in some cases here, they were surrogate children, but isn't it the same in the homes of parents who have pets? Don't some of them treat their pets as if they were children, and some of them not?

GORDON, 32, MICROSOFT PROGRAMMER

Gordon has been married 6 years to Sandy who is a 32-year-old homemaker. His family is Catholic, hers Methodist. They live in Redmond, Washington.

Tell me about your decision and how your families have reacted.

Before we were married, we decided we weren't going to have children for 5 years. Then at the 4-year mark, the decision basically was a two-sentence conversation, something like, "I guess we're not going to have children," and "I agree." Sandy has fears that she's inherited a lot of emotional baggage from her parents that she doesn't want to pass on.

A lot of guys like me believe it's not really up to them. You could have children, you could not have children. Men just want to do whatever makes the relationship work. It's a form of apathy. When I was growing up I had no ideas about having children. I hoped I would get married and that's about all the hopes I ever had. And I did, so I'm satisfied.

My mom talked to Sandy about it, she's very open-minded and Sandy told her we probably weren't going to have children. My dad is a lot like me. He's a computer programmer too. We don't talk a lot about emotional stuff, and the decision of whether or not to have children is a very emotional thing, so I imagine he just doesn't think about it. My sister has told Sandy, "Oh, no, you should have kids, they're so great," but Sandy doesn't go for it. My friends with children tell me they get all these special moments with their kids that are so wonderful, but I don't see that as them trying to convince me.

Tell me what it means to be happy just as you are.

I like to be intellectual, thinking and analyzing and figuring out what the best choice is of those available. We're luckily in a situation where we have extra money, and right now I'm trying to assess my level of risk. How much of it am I willing to lose? I can risk losing most of it because I could do what I do for a long time. I have a lot of insurance for Sandy should something happen to me. I get bonuses and stock options and they've gone up so much in value that now it's very scary because 7 years ago I had nothing at all. Another thing is I don't want to be grown up all the time. Sandy and I can be impulsive, go to a movie like that, go for a walk like that, go on vacation like that.

How many hours do you work a day? What's your average week?

I do two types of work and my job has two periods of time. There's the planning and designing period of time that takes a lot of brain power but little actual work goes on. Then there's the implementation phase when you're producing some Microsoft product. When that's going on, it's hell. Sixteen-hour days, 7 days a week. The longest time I worked like that was a whole year. Never a day off. Seven days a week from 10:00 in the morning until 2:00 in the morning. We were rewarded with stock options and bonuses, but as soon as it was over I got a different position where I have more control over the design phase, but I still work 12-hour days.

Okay, tell me why you aren't attracted to children.

I don't want eighteen years of, "Oh, no, I have to be responsible for you, teach you and train you and do all the things that have to be done." I don't like kids screaming in a restaurant or movie or kids going out and vandalizing. I only like children who are very well-behaved, and I know that's a character flaw because I'm judging these kids. But I like my character flaw, and I couldn't cope if I had a child who misbehaved.

Another thing is I value my time with my wife and secondly, she would not like to share me with children. Because she would have to take care of them while I was away, and when we were together she'd have to manage *them and me*, and she has enough trouble managing me.

I wish I had more time for things away from work. I'm not meeting my goals, except the major one of making sure that Sandy doesn't have to work unless she wants to. My time after work is very precious to me and I want to spend it doing things that Sandy likes to do, and being peaceful, quiet, and relaxing. She likes to travel, but my attitude toward travel is, I'd like to visit the Smithsonian, but I'd rather the Smithsonian came to me.

Did your relationship with your parents or sister have
anything to do with your decision?

For Sandy, it has to do with her mother. For me, maybe my sister. Sandy's mother first tried to force her into a career. Sandy's rebellion was to say, "I'm not going to be forced into a career. I'm going to do what I want to do." Now there's lots of talk over the phone about, "You should have children." I've asked Sandy, "Don't you think the way you feel about children is a reaction to your mother?" and she believes her imprint of what she'd be like as a mother she got from her mom and she rejects it.

For me I saw my sister have a child at 13 and it should have been a good thing, bringing a child into the world, but she was stereotyped as another irresponsible teenager. It wasn't a loving, comfortable experience for her. She had to change schools, get special education so people wouldn't know she was pregnant.

When she was growing up, she rebelled a lot. She smoked, ran away. When her daughter got to her teenage years and started rebelling, she got so mad. Parents see their children as extensions of themselves. I tried to tell her that what was happening to her was exactly what she had done to our parents. What does she say back but, "I still think I'm right in raising her the way I am."

Is Ben's choice of a home in the country with a nondemanding job a way of handling stress? He acknowledges that he has a problem with depression and that the charged pace of San Francisco didn't help. Likewise, Murray consciously avoids the stress he sees co-workers get themselves into and takes off in his RV every chance he gets. Last, Gordon copes with the stress of his job by not trying to handle anything more than quiet time with Sandy.

I hadn't realized that men cared so much about their homes, cooking, gardening, sharing domestic routines. I guess homes are like relationships, women talk about them more than men, but men care just as much when home represents a haven from the stresses of the work world. Domestic tranquility definitely was one of the advantages these men enjoyed even though they'd rather talk about how impulsive they can be—to go out to dinner, go to a movie, go on vacation.

Chapter 6

Avoiding Mistakes

> When children do badly as they enter adult life, men feel the dismay of personal failure. . . . They will, of course, have devoted time and thought and energy to the child. If, despite all this, the child continues to do badly, the men can become angry and bitter. . . . Because men feel responsible for sponsoring their children into adulthood, they blame themselves if the child goes wrong. . . . Even when men feel that they did their best, they can blame themselves for not having done better. (Robert Weiss, 1990, pp. 185-187)

Who is Dr. Weiss talking about? A group of successful, upper-middle class American males, over a third of whom felt that they had failed their children. This struck Dr. Weiss as a very large proportion, and I agreed.

Two types of disappointment with being a father also have been described by another psychiatrist, Terry Kupers (1993). The first disappointment is what Weiss found: "The father is disillusioned when the son fails to become the man he had envisioned. Sometimes it helps for the father to recall his own passage into adulthood, and consider the ways in which he was a disappointment to his father. Or the father might look into his own motives for wishing his son will turn out to be a certain kind of man—is he expecting his son to live out some of his unfulfilled aspirations?" (p. 101)

The second kind of disappointment was news to me: Sons are just as disappointed with their fathers. Sons' disillusionment is so widespread that Kupers regards it as a "normal developmental event."

Because these two therapists who work with men had found extensive disillusionment with the father role in both fathers and sons, I wanted to ask about fear of failure in rearing children. But being aware of how sensitive the average man is to the "F-word," as it is known, I instead used "disappointment" in the Reasons Exercise. Disappointment points no finger of blame. You can be disappointed with an outcome without assuming you caused it. Don't we all get disappointed sometimes by our partners, friends, neighbors, colleagues? Why not our children?

DENIAL OF DISAPPOINTMENT

Even "disappointment" proved too strong a word for the interviewees. Possible disappointment was the primary motive of just one man. Equally significant, eleven men interviewed said that the prospect of disappointment was *least* like them. Why?

Well, the men said, if they had chosen to be fathers, they would have given it 150% and done it right. They would have accepted their children as they were. They would have sacrificed, done whatever it took in terms of time and money, to ensure their kids turned out all right. Failure and disappointment didn't come into it. Dr. Weiss said, "Even when men feel that they did their best, they can blame themselves for not having done better." Not this group. They felt that if you did your best, you couldn't possibly feel you might have done better.

Sometimes I challenged the men. Why are you denying for yourself the disappointment you see around you all the time, every day, in your own family, in the families of your workmates, in your next door neighbors, in society as a whole? Most could not begin to contemplate such a possibility.

THE NEED TO SUCCEED

I asked Phil, geography teacher and world traveler, to explain why possible disappointment was such an unpopular motive.

It's a male thing. When men make a decision, it's going to work. That's why they made the decision. To someone who thinks like me, of course, there's the possibility you'll be disappointed. It's common sense that things aren't always going to go the way you want. Particularly for young men, these items imply that they're ineffectual or a bit stupid to take on something that they knew they couldn't succeed in. They see it as an implied insult. The role of the male is very important to young men, to go out and make that living and bring up that family right. Even to young men who have decided not to.

Root Cartwright, head of BON, commented:

It's defensive drivel. If you've made a firm decision not to become a parent, how can you say at the same time, "but if I had, I would have made a success of it"? It makes no sense to me. If I were to draw up a list of reasons why I've never wanted to have kids, fear of failure is very definitely amongst those reasons. Because you only get one shot at it. If you fuck up childrearing, that's it. Even people who make a first-rate job of it are not entirely free of the fear of failure in their parenting.

Yet here is computer programmer Gordon, whose sister had a baby at age 13, saying:

I have no doubts about how good a father I'd be; I'd be successful. The divorce statistics are everybody else, not me. It could be 99% get divorced but I'm the 1%. I would have paid as much attention to childrearing as I could have and done the best I could. For example, all children go through a rebellious phase where they want to be separated from their family. That's going to happen, and if I had a child and got to that point, I would love that time. Because I would talk with the child and give my perspective on rebellion and help the child rebel in a productive way. I would never, never live my life through my child.

Jane Bartlett writes about the "self-confessed bad mothers" among her childfree women. When asked, do you have the skills, reserves, and personal attributes to cope well with motherhood, many said no. They didn't have the patience or energy. They would be overanxious and overprotective. They hated the noise, the mess, the constant chaos. Many said they could not stand losing control over their lives. Only a minority said they would have been "good enough mothers."

It's no accident that Graham was told (in Chapter 1) "My child was a mistake" by a young mother, not a young father. As Ben Greenstein (1993) says: "The drive to succeed is so deeply imprinted on the male psyche that it is virtually a biological need. . . . Success means different things to different men. It may be the attainment of wealth, fame, power, women or intellectual status or the whole bangshoot. But whatever the aim, the unifying principle is the need to associate himself with and be recognized by other successful men, and to distance himself from failure and those who fail" (pp. 118-119).

SIMON, 44, GUITAR TEACHER

One man was motivated from early childhood not to repeat the failed childrearing he saw around him. Simon lives in Seven Oaks south of London with Jane, age 40, his partner of 2 years, who is a university lecturer. Simon comes from a lower middle-class, Catholic family and is one of six children. He teaches at an inner-city London school and is now a Buddhist.

Tell me about your decision.

I was aware of the disappointments in my own family from as early as I can remember having thoughts. It goes way, way back. There's an assumption underlying your exercise that having children is a natural, normal thing that we're destined to do, whereas it's always been natural to me *not* to have children. When I was 8, I became aware of what people's lives outside my family were like, and I started having opinions about how people should relate to each other. So my attitude toward responsible relationships goes back as far as I can remember.

My parents had very little that was civil between them and an awful lot that was downright aggressive. When I was 9 I spent as much time outside the family home as possible. I remember being on a school walking trip in Belgium and a good friend of mine said how homesick he was. It was a concept I couldn't begin to fathom. Someone had to explain to me what homesick meant.

The first discussion I had was 24 years ago, when I had a partner who was keen to have children. I told her we were too young, had no stable jobs, we were floating around where we lived. Then I had two relationships with women who already had children. The time and energy they required was considerable. The kids suffered from their mothers' ongoing problems with their fathers.

Now I'm with Jane, and one of the things we have in common is that she, too, has no interest in having children. She's an academic and her career is really taking off, which is a great delight.

Do your parents know of your decision?

I don't have a particularly communicative relationship with my father. He and my mother divorced when I was 10. The three oldest of us went to live with him and the three youngest went with my mother. My mother knows of my decision and she thinks it's positive because our whole family's success rate at raising children is pretty bad. None of us were planned. Their relationship was absolutely dreadful, and they've spoken only once since the divorce.

I'm convinced for myself and for everybody I know intimately that we can't escape the influences of our family. We're simply destined to repeat them. I see it happening over and over again. My brothers and sisters all have children, terrible relationships with their spouses, and unfortunate, awkward relationships with their children.

My dad was an extremely frustrated and angry man, verbally and physically. He hit us all quite regularly without much reason, shouted, threw things around. But he was quite good financially, changed his job only once, moved house only once. So, yeah, he was dutiful and responsible. My childhood was stable compared to my siblings' who lived with my mother. She lived in fifteen homes in 5 years and had a pretty crazy life.

So you see why I'd have doubts about how good a parent I'd be. I took after my father in being quite driven professionally. I would get very frustrated when things didn't go the way I wanted.

This is why the main reason for your decision was being disappointed?

I knew there was anger and frustration in me that, inevitably, would be expressed in intimate relationships. My anger at my partners has diminished hugely over the years as I've learned how to be in a relationship and what it means. We only learn to be in relationships with others and with ourselves through diligent effort. That's what attracted me to Buddhism.

I'd make far better parent material now than I would have 20, or 15, or 5 years ago, but my desire to have children has not increased with my ability to do it. My friends have been involved in having children for quite a long time and I've been quite concerned for them and their children over the years. The idea of anybody doing a responsible job of it seems more and more remote as I've seen the failures. Also, I teach children with emotional and behavioral difficulties and 99 percent of them come from tragically awful families where all kinds of abuse is the norm. Nevertheless, as sex education is cut in schools, each year we have a higher percentage of pregnancies among the children and most of them want to keep their children.

You've also said that your relationship with Jane is very important.

Yes, it all actually started 10 years ago when I began what has become a very important relationship with an elderly couple who are childless. He was 70 then, she was 65, and they had made the decision not to have children. I was excited to meet people who were so actively involved in their own lives. As a result of being childless, their interests could spread out and be shared with other people. They were still trying to make sense of their lives. There wasn't a cut-off point, as there seems to be for a lot of people. I've never known anybody married that long, and it was fascinating to talk to them about the responsibility they had toward the relationship.

I want what they have. Despite the fact that Jane's very successful in the academic world, her mother would be happier if she worked in a florist's, was raising children, and lived in suburban Essex across the street from her. Jane continues to put a worrying amount of energy into her relationship with her mother. Her career has been, from an early age, a refuge from her own family, especially her smothering mother.

I've got another relationship reason. I'm part of a very large family and another reason for deciding on not having children is simply because the world needs a few people around in these extended families who can shoulder some of the burden. I've got five siblings with children whom I support emotionally and occasionally financially. I have the time and I have some income. My mother has practically no income, my sisters practically none. My brothers take no interest in the rest of the family.

Tell me why preserving your identity is part of your decision.

I want to keep the time I now have for meditation. I meditate an hour a day on my own, read a lot, go to a couple evening meetings a week, and every

6 weeks I spend a week on silent retreat, in lots of different places. It's a monastic tradition. You go to bed at 10:00, get up at 4:00. There is some teaching at 6:00 in the morning and 6:00 at night. Two mealtimes, a breakfast early in the morning and lunch at 11:00. The idea is that meditation can permeate all aspects of life so there is an eating meditation, a meditation on the bowels. It's about constant mindfulness, being completely aware in the moment, and not getting caught up with thoughts of the past and the future. The meditation is being utterly focused on one activity, whatever activity that might be. When we're doing the dishes, we're doing the dishes.

Through Buddhism I am struggling with various existential questions. The tragedies of society are endless and endlessly repeated. Perhaps the tragedies are just as much a part of life as the seeming successes. Coming to terms with that is the most important thing. Buddhist striving is not towards intellectual answers, but towards experiential understanding, wisdom which is beyond the intellect.

Control is not important to you. Explain.

I put very little energy into planning for the future. One of the lessons of my past is that the future is never what I expect it to be. Money's not an issue for me either. My previous career as a performing musician was absolutely predicated on success in the future, and when I gave up that career 6 years ago, I started living—if not in the moment—at least for this month. I was a determined careerist, and when I questioned that this might not end with a pot of gold at the end of the rainbow, the question of what next was terrifying. I do have a mortgage for the first time. This place is my old-age insurance. By the time I'm retired, I can sell it and move into a small hut somewhere in the woods and live off the proceeds.

Do you think childfree men have to deal with masculinity issues?

I haven't had to. But I see it happen to the children I teach. These 15 to 16-year-old young men, and their partners of similar age, come from very deprived backgrounds. Their potential for proving themselves in any sphere, other than criminal, is direly limited. This is an inner-city, working-class, no-hope population. The men exhibit the same attitude toward having a baby as their partners do. They hold it up and say, "Look what I've achieved." Show it off to their friends and family and get lots of attention. For these men it does have something to do with virility. They're given some status as fathers. Otherwise they have no status at all. It's another of those tragedies of society that is endlessly repeated.

It's no mystery why Simon, who lives in the moment, rejects as a reason for not having children to maintain control over the future. What about the rest of the men? Having control over their lives was not a reason they gave for not having kids, whereas the literature on childfree women emphasizes this motive. I mentioned earlier in this chapter that Jane Bartlett writes about it, as does Leslie Lafayette in *Why Don't You Have Kids?*

BOB, 53, UTILITIES ENGINEER

Bob has been in the utility industry for 21 years. His wife of 19 years, Judy, 48, is a certified mental health counselor. Bob's family was lower-middle class and Catholic. Bob and Judy live in a waterfront cottage on Whidbey Island, northwest of Seattle, and regularly take the ferry to the mainland and their jobs.

Tell me about your decision and how others have reacted to it.

It was one of those nondecisions. I never really wanted children. It always surprised me when other men said they were going to have them. It was like, "Oh, why?" Nonetheless, I assumed it would happen one day but it never did, and I've never felt we needed to do anything about it. My life's pretty complete. Until I was through graduate school and into my first job, maybe 27 years old, I never even thought about children.

My mom told Judy that she wanted to be a grandmother, but we hadn't been married very long when she died. Had she lived I might have felt some obligation to have children because it would have hurt her for me not to have kids. She would have thought there was something missing in my life and I would have been embarrassed not having children and letting her down. Mom knows best, no matter how old you get. At least that's what they tell you.

Every once in a while at work I get asked, "Why don't you have children?" I say, "Just lucky, I guess." It throws them for a loop. I had a good friend I went to graduate school with who got married and had a little girl, and when he came out to visit from the East, all he did was talk about his daughter. He left saying that we didn't have anything in common anymore because I didn't have children. I felt, "Why can't we still be friends?" But he dropped out of my life. Now, after all these years, we're getting back together again. His daughter flunked ninth grade so they're sending her to this special school 3,000 miles from home to get her back on the right track. It hurts me to see them send her away like that. I don't know how he's going to afford it because he just got laid off, after 20 years with his company.

You've said that fear of disappointment didn't affect your decision. Tell me about that.

If I had really wanted kids when I was younger, the likelihood of disappointment wouldn't have paralyzed me. I'd have said, "Yeah, bad outcomes can happen, but I hope they won't." Because the possible disappointment was so far in the future, I'd have thought that it wasn't a big enough risk.

Today I see that no matter what you do, children can disappoint you. I certainly think my children could have disappointed me. Families have four kids, three of them are great and one of them's a total fuckup. How do you keep a kid from having spina bifida? From being born with some horrible kind of birth defect? Kids are human. You can help and direct and guide, but you can't guarantee an outcome. They can get into trouble. It's like with decision analysis at work. I can help people make good decisions, but I cannot guarantee good outcomes.

Sometimes I think that if we'd had children, I might not have been such a good father. I might have been too isolated, too distant, cold, too much like my dad. The worst was feelings of abandonment. My dad and I were on a trip, staying in a hotel, and he went out when I was sleeping one morning and I woke up in this strange room by myself. My parents put me on a train once at Christmas to visit my grandparents but my grandparents never got the letter saying I was coming, so there I was at 5 years old with no one to meet me in the dead of winter. Every summer they sent me to a farm where there were no children, just a great uncle and aunt. This is the first time I've had to think about my shitty childhood in relation to not feeling a need for a family. They could be very much related.

For some reason it's been easier to be angry with my dad than my mother, so I'm still struggling with my mother's role in their fending me off. But I am beginning to see the duplicity of my mother in this whole thing.

My dad's still alive and our relationship is formal and superficial, the way it's been my whole life. Our conversations are very factual, never about feelings or emotions. Never were, never will be.

Why was preserving your identity important?

I'm happy as I am. I love to learn things and at work I do a lot of computer modeling and simulation, various techniques for making decisions. That's what I really like to do, decision analysis. It's a neat integration of mathematics and dealing with people, taking people's subjective ideas and finding ways to quantify them. I don't know what I could do that would be more pleasurable than my job.

You've indicated that job freedom is important to you.

Right now my company is merging with another and we're going through the downsizing that is like so much of corporate America today, and I am consciously aware that I would have a lot more worries if I had children. If I lose my job, or if we have to sell this house, Judy and I can deal with it. I had talked to my boss about the possibility of working at home a day or two a week, and in the long run it's doable. But right now, with the merger and downsizing, he said, "You're better off coming in and being visible." Another advantage is the possibility of retiring earlier. I don't like getting up at 6:00 in the morning in the winter to drive to work. If I could consult from home and focus on what I really like to do, I can see retirement sometime in the next 10 years.

We got married fairly late and if we'd had kids, they'd be going to college about now and at the maximum-consumption-of-money age. I would be forced to stay in a job even if I didn't like it. My mom believed in education so much that while I was in the Navy, even though she was in her 50s, she went back to school to become a LPN so she could work to send me to college.

Tell me why having time for yourself was so important.

I have a tendency toward depression. That's the thing that scares me most about having children, not having time when I need to get away and find isolation. If you're a parent, you've got to be up all the time. I have trouble enough in my marriage with this. I'm in counseling to deal with my need to withdraw.

I've always liked doing things by myself. I love to take our little sailboat off by myself. I like to hike alone. I don't feel that I would like to share those times with children. I like my hobbies—backpacking, climbing, model trains, and the cats. I dearly love them. Once we had six pets, three dogs and three cats, and somebody made a comment, "Oh, these are your children," so I decided then and there, "No, they are just pets." But we do spend a lot of money on them. One stray dog we picked up immediately had $1,200 worth of eye surgery. So there is deep caring for the animals, but they're not child substitutes. When this dog died a year ago, that was the first time in 20 years we didn't have at least one dog, but we like the freedom of not having a dog. Cats you can leave in the care of a pet sitter who comes over and feeds them.

Fathers' connections with their sons' decisions not to have children are taken up in Chapter 13. Bob's dad is classified as "disinterested." Bob can hardly bear to see self-absorbed fathers brush off their children in the park, in stores, on the ferry. He'd like to clobber the men but gets depressed instead.

GRAHAM, 32, PHARMACEUTICAL SALESMAN

Graham is married to 28-year-old Janet who is a freelance greeting card illustrator. They live in the north of England and Graham had joined his present employer only a month before our interview. His decision-making process was featured in Chapter 1.

Freedom was most important to you. Talk about that.

I travel a lot in my profession and I can do so without wondering how my wife and child are coping at home without me. It's also the lifestyle of avoiding the routines children impose. "Would you like to go to the pub tonight, dear?" and we're off. Or it might mean a walk out on the heath, a drive down the road, a film, a quiet evening in front of the telly. Life as an adult.

I earn quite a lot of money, but there's a lot of risk tied up with the job of a salesman. It means working long hours and if I don't hit the target, well, you know. One of the spontaneous things it is nice to do is return from a business trip with a couple of tickets to go on Eurostar, or for a plane, and say to the wife, "We're going away for the weekend." That's the kind of impulsive gesture that keeps our relationship alive. I also go off and spend weekends at the houses of old friends without worrying that my wife is going to resent me for buggering off and leaving her holding the baby, literally.

We love long walks, pub lunches, socializing, that sort of stuff. Our dog and cats are trained to go in kennels when we're away, which is part of our refusal to be restricted. We're both cooks. We cook together or apart or for each other. Something that we're very keen to do is buy a plot of land and build a house, which is going to take a heap of money. In 10 years I'll have saved enough from my salary to pay for the whole thing because I'm not forking out £10,000 a year on a child.

You very strongly resist the responsibilities involved in raising a child.

If you could get a child from incontinence to independence in 5 years, it might be worth considering. I have a friend with a couple of kids and he says, "I love them dearly, but you can't give them back and there are times when it would be quite nice to." Maybe that's why boarding schools are doing a good business, even in these days. I'd never do that. One of the reasons I decided not to become a parent is that I have a very realistic idea of the responsibility involved. Another is wanting to avoid a mistake.

There's this poem by Philip Larkin that begins, "They fuck you up, your mum and dad." It goes on about how they may not intend it but they give you their faults, and extra ones besides. So the concomitant of all the assets you have to pass on is, you may also be carrying around a load of crap and you give your children the best part of that, too. Why?

Because you haven't got the time, you're tired, you're stressed, you've got other things on your mind, and your child comes and shows you this lovely painting. "Look Daddy, what I did for you." But he's caught you in a bad moment and you push him away and growl, "Later." This was a fundamental point in that child's life. It's that kind of stuff a parent's got to be aware of all the time and that's the legacy you're leaving them. Never mind your good intentions. How you are is how they end up.

And your job is also very important?

I want to retire early. Once we've built the house and there's no mortgage or rent to pay, then I'm no longer committed to working however many hours to earn however much money.

My father is 64 and he wants to retire, but he can't because he's got to put my little brother through university. That's his responsibility, so tough. I don't want to find myself in that situation. I'll be free to do something else like a carpenter or fisherman, it doesn't matter what. The important thing is that I'll be free to choose rather than be boxed in a corner where I have to earn £35,000 a year for the next 40 years.

I've heard that companies are biased towards "family men" and against childfree men. What do you think?

I don't think bias will be an issue. The job I do is fairly solitary, a low contact kind of job. I'm only in the office 1 day a week. If I had an office job 5 days a week, I might lose something in empathy. Because whoever your boss is, or whoever his boss is, they talk about their families and children and sending them to university. If you say, "Well, I haven't got children," some people will take that as an implicit criticism.

I'm also protected because promotion is not something I want. I did want it at one time, but not anymore. Now I want the freedom that comes from having the money to buy land, build on it, and travel. Success at my job comes from simply going out and selling. But I would never let myself get in a situation where my future was in the hands of an employer who was biased against me for not having children. I'd switch companies.

The notion of preserving your identity didn't come into it?

I'm never satisfied. I'm a chameleon. I prefer change.

You'll meet up next with Graham in Chapter 13 where he describes a common complaint: poor father-son commmunication.

A MATURE POINT OF VIEW?

Perhaps Frank, systems analyst and Manchester marathoner, was right when he said, "Fear of disappointment is a mature point of view. In terms of other people's children, it's only now that I see the problems my colleagues have. At the time I decided not to have children, these things weren't applicable."

Avoiding disappointment as a motive, interestingly, does coincide with why 70% of Ann Landers' readers who, when asked what they would change if they had their life to live over again, said they would not have children. In addition to overpopulation concerns, the other reasons came from parents who said their children had ruined their marriages, older parents who sacrificed too much, and parents whose teenagers were in trouble (Veevers, 1980, p. 123). These motives are all from a mature point of view.

Glenn, a childfree, 61-year-old retired Portland economist, reflected:

Kids represent one more thing to have to worry about, forever. I don't think there is a family I know of, with more than one kid, in which somebody hasn't turned out to be a real source of anxiety. Parents my age have been parenting so long, they don't know how to stop. The kids keep coming around and reminding them of their inadequacies as parents and their inadequacies as children.

There is a very high probability that you aren't going to be a successful parent, no matter who you are, or what resources you have, or how hard you try. Even if children are not overtly in trouble, whatever they do, they can't do it right from the parent's point of view. They can't live close enough, or visit enough. They can't marry the right person, or go to the right school, or take the right degree, or get the right job, or live in the right place. Nor can they behave toward you exactly as you would want them to behave.

I don't have those worries. The most I worry about is what's going to happen tomorrow in my life. I certainly don't have to worry about anyone in the sense of, "Am I responsible for them?" Or, "Are they behaving towards me like I have a right to expect?" There's no one out there that has those sorts of claims on me.

Robert Weiss (1990) inspired this chapter, along with what we all recognize—rearing kids ain't what it used to be. In previous generations, people could have the worthy goal of giving children the advantages they didn't have, and sending them off into the world to do the great things that they couldn't do. There were traditional roles to be fulfilled: Men provided, women nurtured, and both had a fair degree of control over the situation. Churches and schools cooperated. They had a chance of being successful. But today, some fathers of grown children admit, as Dr. Weiss's men did, that they failed in bringing up their kids. And their childfree peers can reflect on the hurt they've been spared.

Chapter 7

Not Liking Kids

At some point in the interviews, respondents were asked outright: "Do you like children?" Virtually everyone, male and female alike, found this query difficult. About half of our respondents were insulted that the question had been asked, and expressed varying degrees of indignation at the imputation of what they perceived to be an abnormality. . . . The other half of our respondents. . . eventually admitted that, in fact, they did not especially like children. Once the statement was made, it was then supported by specific instances of the dislike either of particular children or, more usually, of particularly childlike traits. (Jean Veevers, 1980, pp. 61-62)

ROGER, 55, SALES MANAGER

Roger works for a building materials company, and has been married 24 years to Nina, a 48-year-old homemaker. He has 2 years of college, and he served as an apprentice to become a joiner. Roger and Nina grew up in Camden, New Jersey, in Catholic families. To escape the heat and humidity of East Coast summers, they moved to Puyallup, Washington, 10 years ago.

Tell me about your decision.

We had been going together for 5 years, trying to talk ourselves out of getting married. We decided that the only way we were going to find out if we wanted to be married was to do it. During that time, whenever the subject of children came up, we both had very definite ideas that we did not want them. As we matured, our insight into *why* has changed. My brother and I were often told by our dad what a bother it was to have kids. My father had a cruel streak in him. He was mentally and emotionally abusive. At a subconscious level I didn't want to do that to a kid. Though that realization has only come to me recently, not in my younger years.

When I was young, children were alien creatures. You can't reason with a screaming baby. When I was growing up and our relatives would have babies, I always felt uncomfortable around them. That feeling's stayed with me.

So you've known a long time that you do not like to be around children.

My patience has a very long fuse, but when I've had enough, I've had enough. I don't mind dealing with children one-on-one for a short period of time, for the good times. But when children become cranky or obnoxious, I don't want anything to do with them. The folks at work know I don't care for misbehaving children, so when the screaming kids come in, everybody gets a big kick out of it teasing me, "RJ, your favorites are coming."

My view of being a father is having the responsibility of providing home, hearth, encouragement, love, support, teaching, training, etc., from the moment of birth until the moment the child leaves on his own. It's an overwhelming task. At work I am required to be very structured, focused, and very intense in my position. So when it's my time, it's my time, and I choose to do what I want to do, even if that means nothing. With a child I would always be on call.

Three years ago we rescued a cat that was run over by a car. I don't know how people who have really sick or injured children manage it. But I know how I felt about this stupid cat. His jaw was broken, and I remember worrying, "Has the cat suffered? How's he gonna eat?" How does a father operate if he has children? I assume you have deeper feelings of affection for a child than for a cat. I've always figured children would complicate your life terribly. That cat has complicated our life. We rescued him and now it's our responsibility to take care of him.

What do you like to do in your free time?

The ultimate vegetative state is to sit and do a crossword puzzle and listen to classical music. I surf the Internet, learn software, read a lot, build models and miniatures of aircraft, ships, trains. I carve freeform objects and throw them away. I'm building cabinets. I rebuilt an engine for my truck. I got a book on how to do it and it took me all winter. Nobody was more surprised that it ran than I was. That's the type of mechanical, manipulative work that I enjoy and that I can't do as a salesman.

My official title is showroom manager. I take care of anyone who walks into the showroom. I answer as many cold sales phone calls as possible. I have a list of 300 clients that I have to take care of, a few big Japanese clients. The company exports building materials to Japan, and their needs are very time-sensitive. Every order that comes in is late already. That's the negative side of the job.

The positive side of the job is I enjoy helping folks fulfill their dreams. It sounds corny, but folks come in building a new home, they don't know what they want, and I can steer them in the right direction. It's physically easier than the construction trade that I was in for 20 years, but I don't get to see the fruits of my labor. Before this job I was a supervisor in a couple of factories making wood products. Again, I was helping people, helping my employees achieve their full potential. But being a supervisor today is so much like being a father. After a while you get tired of being the confessor and the disciplinarian, and I had to get away from it.

You're not the only childfree man I've talked to who doesn't want to be grown up all the time.

The day I grow up it's time to put me in a casket. I like to do silly things, let myself go when I want to. Getting in the car and going to the Wooden Boat Festival and getting totally immersed in playing with wooden boats. Enjoying the childlike wonder of discovery by looking through a telescope at a distant planet. I get a soul-satisfying feeling coming to work some mornings when Mt. Rainier is sitting out there and has a certain pink aura about it when the sun is below the horizon and just glinting off the snow. We like going to the Oregon Museum of Science and Industry in Portland. It's set up for kids. I knock myself out going in there and having a ball with them. I don't know if I could do that as a father.

I'm shocked when I realize how old I am. My God, you're 55 years old. Wow. Inside I feel somewhere between 20 and 40. Nina feels the same. She's active in Toastmasters and in the county extension homemakers organization.

As far as your job's concerned, what do you value most?

The freedom to change. If I'm working at a job I detest, but it's my choice because I'm too apprehensive or lazy to find a better job, that's a choice I make and that's okay. But if I'm working at a job I detest because I don't want to quit for fear of losing medical benefits or not making enough money to support a family, that's a heavy burden. I know I can't walk into work and just quit, but there's the illusion of being able to tell my boss to take a flying leap.

Not being able to care for children financially is an overriding consideration with me. Being a father is a pretty scary proposition. Even today I don't know if I have the self-assurance to be a good father. I've done other things I didn't have much self-confidence for, but they were transient, like learning to fly and to play the piano.

What's your attitude toward not leaving a legacy to your children?

I've left a legacy in over 300 homes that I have built. In every house that I worked on, I signed my name on that house, somewhere, up in the roof, in the rafters. I put the year, my name, and a pithy political comment. I went back to New Jersey a year ago, after ten years. I went around and took photographs of many of the homes that I built there. That's my legacy for future generations.

Men find it easier to say they don't like kids than women. Compared to 26% of women giving dislike as a reason for remaining childless, 46% of men did so. Sociologist Sharon Houseknecht (1987) speculates that the reason for the difference may be simply that it's less culturally acceptable for women to admit this. On the other hand, it is my guess that disproportionately fewer childfree men than childfree women work professionally with children, which is also true in the general population. Certainly, comparing this group of men with the women interviewed by Terri Casey (1998) and Carolyn Morell (1994), childfree women enjoy children far more than childfree men.

WALTER, 42, NURSING INFORMATICS LECTURER

Walter lectures on technology and nursing in a School of Health and Social Welfare. He has been married 10 years to Constance, a 34-year-old consultant in clinical oncology. They met on the wards when he was a student nurse and she was a medical student. Walter is the oldest of seven children born in York into a working-class Church of England family. His grandmother was a nurse, his father a psychiatric nurse, his mother a homemaker.

Tell me about your decision, what might have influenced it, and other people's reactions.

Before we got married, neither of us particularly wanted children. After we'd been married 7 years, we were still firmly convinced, and we decided against continuing the pill and other contraceptive means. I went to the vet, as it were, in 1994 to have a vasectomy.

As far as family reactions, my parents are dead, and I'm not particularly close to my brothers or sisters. My relationship with my father wasn't close, although he wasn't distant or cold, that end of the spectrum. He kept an eye on what we did, but was more willing than a lot of parents to let us learn from our mistakes.

Outside the family, people *wonder* why you don't have children, but only one or two of them ever have *asked* why. I simply said that I don't want them. When we were first married, we'd tell others, "We don't want any children at this point, but we may change our minds." We *did* change our minds: We came to a firmer decision that we didn't want them.

I may have been influenced by being the eldest. Since my mid-teens, I did the shopping locally for the family and I would always take one or the other of my younger brothers or sisters along. I took them to the park as well, just to get some of us out of the house. My father's parents lived with us, and with so many people in one household it was difficult to find time and space on your own.

You've indicated that you are not at all attracted to children. Elaborate.

I find children wearing after not quite milliseconds. When I'm with my sisters and brothers, there's always the expectation that I'll want to pick their babies up and fuss over them. I do it for show and get rid of them as quickly as possible.

Now, obviously when I was doing my nurse training, I was on a pediatrics ward for 8 weeks with children of various ages. I was quite happy to look after those children. It was an employment situation and I was free of them when I walked out the door at the end of the shift.

I've known how I felt about children ever since I left home and went to university. I have an attitude similar to Captain Picard in *Star Trek: The Next Generation*. This man doesn't like children. Once on holiday in Kenya there was a couple with a small baby in the next room, and the baby started screaming and I was getting ready to go hammer on the door, when an elderly German woman ran down the corridor and started banging, "I come out on holiday for peace and quiet, not for your baby to keep me awake all night." We like to go on holiday a couple of times a year and having children would severely restrict that. We've had short breaks to Paris, Barcelona, Budapest. For longer holidays, we've gone to Egypt, Tenerife, the other Canary islands, Granada, our favorite place. So the holiday issue did influence our decision.

From your childhood I can understand why time and
space on your own are important. Tell me more.

The variety and range of things that I'm involved in keep me busy and happy. I actually should step back and weed out some of them because I'd like to do more cycling and photography and gardening. My job, my part-time PhD studies, the projects I'm involved in as part of the job, are taking up all my time. I go to several conferences a year, including the annual one at Rutgers University in New Jersey on Nursing Informatics, that's the use of computers in clinical nursing, nursing research, and nursing education. I'm on the advisory board and do a lot of writing for *Health Informatics*, and I also write for *Nurse Education Today, Complexity and Chaos in Nursing,* and *Nursing Standard* on-line.

I spend a lot of time reading. Ever since I was a child I've always had half a dozen books a week out of the library. My most recent interest is in English translations of modern Arabic and Middle-Eastern literature, particularly Naguib Mahfouz, the Egyptian Nobel prize-winning author. My wife and I are these strange people who take Stephen Hawking's *A Brief History of Time* or a book on quantum physics to read on holiday.

You're clearly very happy with your current situation.

I am, but there's a strong financial element to it. If we didn't have the income level that we have, I wouldn't have this freedom to do the things that I want to do when I want to do them. If I want a book, I can afford to buy it. If I want CDs, I buy them.

Tell me why you have expressed no need to be in control of your life.

Look at all the changes in direction I've had in my life so far. Consequently, I don't want to plan too rigidly. Long-term planning, yes, we have been planning for retirement since we got married. There's another aspect to control that is also *not* a need of mine. I don't see myself as someone who wants to have control over people, you know, in a managerial role. Having ideas and trying to implement them because I think they'd be beneficial is what I do, but I draw a line between that and exercising power over other people.

Two guys in a row who don't like to be managers. They weren't the only ones. It has to do with the "responsibility factor"—subordinates, like children, are too dependent, relying on you to tell them how to behave and what's right, what's wrong. They expect you to be supportive and not harsh with your criticism. They tell you their problems and expect you to help them get ahead with life. Responsibility for others and over others is too much for these guys.

STEVE, 37, AIRPLANE PAINTER

Steve has been married 7 years to Sylvia, age 35, a coffee company executive. Both are college graduates from middle-class Protestant homes. They live in Olympia, Washington.

Tell me about the decision.

I kept thinking someday I would want to be a parent. The years rolled by and I never got the urge. Sylvia was taking the pill and said, "Look, I don't want children, and there's a risk of breast cancer if I stay on it for too many years." So 5 years ago I had a vasectomy.

It puzzles me that some parents are offended by my choice. I'm very tolerant about other people's decisions to have children, but when I say there are too many people on the earth, I've had fathers say that I must hate them because they've got three kids. Or they'll ask me if I don't feel something's missing from my life? And I say, "Do you have your pilot's license? Can you do anything you want this weekend? Or the weekend after? We've all got things missing from our lives."

You've said that the freedom to come and go as you please is paramount.

I feel I can have anything I want, not tangibly, but emotionally and spiritually. It's unlimited. All I have to do is go get it. I don't expect it from anyone or anything. I don't need it from children. At this point I have only a couple early goals left that I want to fulfill. Then I'll have to get some new goals because I'm too young be self-actualized.

The two goals are skydiving from a cliff and climbing Mount Everest. I've already done 238 sky dives so the cliff jump's easy, but climbing Everest, I've got to come up with $65,000 and train pretty intensively for it. I'm building an airplane down in the garage, that's going to take at least a year. It's a three-seat, 180 horsepower, all metal. I've climbed the five major peaks in Washington, I'm a rock-climbing instructor, I've built two kayaks, and we sea kayak a lot. We're going to spend at least a week this summer in the San Juan Islands in Canada. I do a lot of mountain biking. I can because I don't have any attachments other than my wife, and she usually beats me to the activity anyway.

We've been to Australia, Europe, China. We fly into a city, rent bikes, and without guides, bicycle all over. This plane I'm building is a bush plane, like a pickup truck with wings. It's got the ability to fly into short fields in remote areas. Sylvia's got a lot of money tied up in stock options, and we're looking to buy twenty acres in Eastern Washington that we can put a small strip on. Then we can ski at Bend or Whitefish on weekend trips with our airplane.

So your major use of time is recreational?

Yup. I want lots of time for my interests. My brother-in-law is an avid flyfisherman, and his wife allows him to fish only one weekend a month. He has to be a father the rest of the time. Sylvia wants more time than I for personal development. She's always taking night classes. Doesn't get home until 10:00 most weeknights. I get more out of how-to books than classes.

She tried to get me to go to Disneyland this past weekend when she took her nephew, but it wouldn't have been any fun for me watching him. I think his parents are the ones who should have been there but they're too busy. I said, "You guys go, have fun, and I'll feel good about that." But I didn't want to be part of it.

Have you always felt this way toward children?

Yes, except when I was a child. I was the one who couldn't stay in his seat and stop bothering other children. Now I see children as I was—out of control and needing a lot of attention to stay out of trouble. There are too many sharp objects and dangerous things around and you can't let 'em out of your sight. Children are juicy little buggers. You go in someone's house who has kids and there's this film of children, saliva, whatever, covering everything. Where is the payoff to put up with the late night feedings, changing diapers, and driving to Little League games? You work your ass off to pay for all this, and the ultimate goal is they go away.

I've just changed jobs, but if I were a parent, I wouldn't have. For 6 years I was an industrial engineer. Then a painting manager asked me to come to work for him, implying there might be a management position in a couple of years. I've made a one hundred eighty degree turn career-wise. There are no promises. I may paint airplanes until I'm 55. I am retiring at 55, have I mentioned that?

Blue collars are let off—last in, first out. If there were a layoff right now, I'd be the first one out the door. But in my salaried job, there was a very high retention rate based on seniority. So if I were a parent, even though I'd much rather work with my hands, I would not have given up that security.

I got a 25% pay increase in the new painting job and it's something else to put on my resume. Wherever I want to go, and Australia's on my mind, the more versatility I've got and the more hirable I'll be.

Tell me why you couldn't possibly have been disappointed in children if you'd had them.

Because if I chose to have children, I would have given it all I could. I don't think I'd be disappointed. If I thought I wasn't doing it right, I'd do something to fix it. I've never failed at anything in life, so I wouldn't have that fear.

If we want to get quantitative about it, sixteen of the men didn't like children, fourteen did. The early articulators tended to dislike children the most, the acquiescers tended to like children the most. Their wives and partners were similarly divided with half not liking kids, half liking them (although almost all the women did not want children of their own). The length of time a childfree man enjoys being around children, or can stand to be with children, gets shorter as he ages. Thus, what might not have been a factor in his earlier decision becomes important with the passage of time.

WHO INITIATES THE CHILDLESS DECISION?

The literature says that since the advent of contraception in Western industrialized countries, it is more often women who initiate the decision not to have children. The literature says that of the four kinds of husband-wife decisions, the most common type is the wife-influential. The other types are husband-influential, independent, and mutual. With so many early articulators among these men, we couldn't expect to find the majority of husband-wife decisions to be wife-led, and they weren't.

Roger and Nina, both early articulators, illustrate the independently made decision. Walter and Constance, both postponers, illustrate the mutually made decision. Steve and Sylvia, another pair of postponers, illustrate the wife-initiated decision. It was Sylvia who brought up the issue of the pill and their obvious disinterest in having children and Steve who supported her. For an illustration of the husband-influential decision, you'll have to move on to Chapter 8, where you'll find an early articulator, Dale, who still has to remind ambivalent Karen of the advantages of only taking care of four cats.

Chapter 8

Early Retirement

There are signs that the early-retirement trend already may have reversed course. In 1950, nearly half of men 65 and older were still working; by 1985, just 16% were. But since then, the rate has remained flat. Many economists believe the numbers soon will begin to tick back upward.

The inescapable reality is that many boomers won't be able to afford to quit working when they hit their 60s. . . . "A lot of 50-year-olds have kids in elementary school," said Stephen Levy, director of the Center for Continuing Study of the California Economy. "You talk about retirement and Arizona, and they look at you like you're from Mars." (Patrice Apodaca, 1998, p. 2)

As many as a third of the men interviewed had thought about early retirement—some because they'd have the wherewithal, some because their occupations were ageist, some because they were looking forward to doing something different. The childfree are notorious for long-range financial planning and the desire to be debt-free, and this bunch was no exception. With the future of work shaping up as it is, if a man truly wants to retire early, he seriously should consider whether to have a child. The first interviewee tells you how.

DALE, 41, RETIRED JAGUAR MECHANIC

Dale earned his early retirement in Los Angeles where he repaired foreign cars for the wealthy. He's been married 18 years to Karen, a 38-year-old mortgage broker who works occasionally from their new home near Seattle to which they moved 2 years ago.

Tell me about your decision.

When I first had a hint that I wanted to be childfree, I was 15 and I'd read a book about zero population growth that made me start to think. Also, my sister had a child whom I babysat a couple of times and it was like, "No, this doesn't appeal to me." Before Karen, I was married for less than a year to a girl I met in high school. She wanted to get married right away and I agreed to that, but shortly after we got married she wanted children. I didn't, so we split up. I was 21.

When I met Karen we had similar interests but she didn't have the same feelings I had about children, so I had to keep showing her the benefits of being childless.

By the time I turned 30 I had got very used to my situation. My parents were older when they had us, in their forties, and it had been hard on them physically to have young children to take care of. We briefly considered adopting a child—a Romanian orphan—rather than add to the planet, but by my mid-thirties I knew for sure it wasn't a good idea.

I'm interested in the sorts of reactions you've gotten from other men.

Most of the time with other men it's like, "Do you have kids?" "No, I don't." "Oh." And that's the end of it. No one ever asks me to my face why. The only person I can think of who made it an issue was an Irish fellow who kept bugging me with "You'll have 'em before you're 30. They really make your life worthwhile." He was from Belfast, Catholic-thinking, and he'd have had a dozen if he hadn't split up with his wife because of his drinking.

You've said you're happy as you are. Tell me more, please.

I want to be able to do whatever I want to do whenever I want to do it. I've been a careful planner all along the way. At the same time I got my first idea about not having children, I also got the idea that I wanted to make as much money in the shortest amount of time that I could and take the rest of my life to enjoy what I had taken the time earlier to accomplish. Early retirement was a goal when I was very young.

I started out as an electronics technician in a computer typesetting place and I didn't like being in a building with no windows. I'd rather be outside, or as close as I could come to it. Cars had always been my hobby. I thought, why not see if I can make money at it? It came naturally to me, and I started making real good money right off the bat.

I worked solely on British sports cars, Rolls Royces and Jaguars. With my electronics background I was able to handle all of the wiring problems British cars are particularly noted for and I loved it.

Some people's idea of retirement is travel. I've never really been that eager to travel. Developing a place like this in the woods is something I've always wanted to do. The money came from savings and the fact that our place in California went up so much in value. I like to do yard work, and with 5 acres I have plenty to keep me busy. We heat the house with wood and I cut all of our firewood. I built that gazebo out there for Karen to keep her birds in. Now that I've got the lawn in, I'll get into landscaping.

You asked me earlier why I had three e-mail addresses. Look at that back room. That's ham radio. It's been around a long time and it has been constantly changing like everything else has been changing. At the time the Internet was developing, ham radio had its own internet. I have a room for my radios and computers, and I'm teaching myself a programming language.

I'm after as simple and uncomplicated a life as possible. I have four cats depending on me and when the fourth one came along, I didn't even know if I could handle that.

You've said not liking children also was a consideration.

I can't stand children for more than a half hour. I'm not parent material. My parents got divorced and my dad left when I was around 11. My mother said to me once, "Don't get this wrong, because it's not that I don't love you, but, believe me, your life will be a lot simpler if you don't have any children." She said this when I was about 14. After that she reminded me several times that if I were to have children, she would not babysit them. I always said, "Don't worry about it, Mom. You won't have to."

I know how much you value time. Tell me what you do with it.

I'm not the kind of person who goes out jogging. I'm the kind of person who does a lot of physical things but not in a structured exercise program. So I want time for exercise and also further education. I'm not taking any college courses, but I'm learning a programming language on my own, through books. I learn a lot of things that way, through reading and applying it.

Every time I find myself accomplishing one thing, I look around and I find there are a lot of other things I want to do. I've got a lot of ham radio things on my mind and I have an old car that's been following me around for 25 years I have to finish. I want to finish the garage, do a pond out there, build a carport and a greenhouse. Karen and I volunteer at a community organic garden once a week. We plant, harvest, weed, dig, exchanging our labor for food.

*You've said you couldn't have been disappointed if you
had been a father.*

I especially don't connect with the idea that divorce is a bad thing. Divorce happens all the time. Nobody's proved that children are worse off if it happens. Frankly, I'm better for it. I was glad when my father left. I got along with my mother much better.

Writers about childfree women often comment that "anybody can be childfree." They mean voluntarily childless women can be found in all educational levels, socioeconomic statuses, occupations, and religions. How many guys like Dale, and Sid, and Carlo from Chapter 1, are out there defying the stereotype that working-class men invariably produce hordes of children?

MATTHEW, 35, GERIATRIC NURSE

Matthew, married 2 years to Rikki, a 31-year-old teacher, plans to be financially independent when he turns 40, in spite of the fact that nurses and teachers don't make very much money. This goal is doubly remarkable inasmuch as Matthew comes from a large, poor Catholic family, left school at 15 with no qualifications, and started work as a grave digger. They live in south London.

Tell me about the decision and how your family has reacted.

I said before we got married that I had never been keen on having children. Sometimes it's an issue, sometimes she's okay about it, sometimes not. In fact, if I knew I was going to die next week, if Rikki wanted to, I'd give her a baby. It wouldn't bother me because I'm not going to be here.

I've never liked noisy kids. That sensitivity's been there as far back as I can remember. If I'm in a supermarket and a parent is hitting their child and it's crying, I say, "Excuse me, would you mind not doing that in front of me?" If they say, "It's none of your business," I say, "You're doing it in front of me, that makes it my business." Babies cry constantly for the first 2 years, and a baby screaming really does my head in.

My mother, who had 5 children when she was age 23, says it's a great pity because I'd make a very good parent. My father thinks I'm off my head, that it's another phase I'm going through, as the black sheep of the family. My sisters' reaction is that I'm too tight. That's the reaction of the female staff at work as well. "Money, that's all you're interested in. What'd you get married for?"

You've said that having time to do what you want is most important. Explain.

I'm doing a course because I want to get a promotion at work. It's a part-time, 2-year course to get a certificate of higher education. I am bitter because I failed the big exam we take when we're 11 years old. I feel the fact that I haven't been educated. Whether I become a lawyer, social worker, or whatever, in time, I want to be educated. The other thing is, I like being in control of my time. I'm the only one on the nursing team that requests every single duty. Because I don't like surprises.

I want more time to travel. Between 1990 and 1991, I went all over the world: America, Mexico, Japan, Australia, Malaysia, Brunei, China, Hong Kong. I have no trouble finding jobs because of the shortage of nurses. Also because I'm willing to work with disabilities, not everybody's cup of tea, and with the elderly mentally infirm, people stuck away in hospitals and nursing homes. Travel-wise I feel trapped at work right now because I'm on this course. But it's a means to a good end.

I got the money to do all that traveling because England has this incredible status symbol thing about number plates. I bought a 1952 Austin stuck in a garage for 17 years for £3,500 with the number plates. I sold the number plates a couple months later for £22,500 because they had these three initials followed by a 1. And they were the initials of this guy who was willing to part with that kind of money.

I need time for exercise. I go to the gym four times a week and I've got gym stuff here as well, weights, punchbag. I can get very steamed up and I can be aggressive, mainly verbally aggressive. I've had one fight in many years, but I still get angry and have a good old whack on the punchbag. I don't like idiots in positions of responsibility. If people are in a position of responsibility, I expect them to fulfill it and if they don't, it makes me mad.

I know that like a lot of childfree guys, you don't want to have to be grown up all the time.

I spend a lot of time talking to people, meeting strangers on the street. New people tend to come into my life every other week. I'm very open and vocal about things and children would suppress my personality. I'm not a conventional English guy walking down the street. I have a lot of eccentric thoughts, and if I had a child I'd have to be grown up and serious and have to suppress this side of my personality.

Rikki and I are happy as we are. If we had a child, our life together, the way we are now, would be finished. A child is like winning the lottery, because you're never, ever going to be the same again. I'm getting so much out of our relationship, selfishly speaking, I'm getting so much love, that I can give so much love. We're together because we choose to be, we want to be, and if we choose not to, we go our separate ways. You can't do that with a child. I've met quite a few men who wish they'd never had children and they'd never do it again.

My personality is such that I don't have the patience to raise kids. No way at all. Even though I'm a nurse and deal with difficult people, I've got the patience for that, but as soon as a kid cried, I'd walk away. As soon as it started being naughty, I'd leave.

I'd like to bring up a child right and proper, but I also know that child is going to do wrong. Society today isn't safe, it's enticing young people to drink, smoke, do drugs, and I'd have very limited control over a child for doing those things.

You've said that money's very important. Tell me more.

We're saving so we can be independent when I'm 40. I own several properties. I used part of the money from the number plates as a deposit on my first house. I lived in a shed in the back garden and rented out every room in the house. I lived on pancakes, rice, and tuna, that was my diet, but I paid the house off within 4 years. The next house was a bargain that has gone way up in value. I rented it out as well, and went to living in the hospital carpark in an ambulance. After that I invested in flats to rent out.

I don't like being in debt. These properties are paying for themselves so that by the time I'm 40, they'll all be paid off. Then I'll be in position to do what I want to do with my wife. We'll be financially secure. Rikki thinks we should open a residential treatment place for underprivileged teenagers, a nice big house in nice surroundings for troubled youths. Because I've had the background that I've had, and the abuse that I've suffered and come through, I think I can use those experiences to help make other children into full potential adults. It's estimated it costs £66,000 to raise one child. That's a hell of a lot of money. I can do a lot more with that money for many children rather than spend it on that one.

I don't understand why being disappointed at childrearing couldn't happen to you.

Well, divorce is not an issue. Do I doubt that I'd be good parent material? No, I'd never hit a child. That's not an issue. I don't have any hangups. I don't drink, don't smoke, don't beat around parties. I've never done drugs. The problem is that society has so many hangups. It's a major reason why I don't want children. I'm a bit of a perfectionist and with a kid, I wouldn't have control over these things. How the hell the Queen copes, I'll never know. The flipping things that she's had to put up with the last 30-odd years. Look at her power and control. She's got the whole country and she can't even control her own kids.

"The voluntarily childless woman finds maternal responsibility almost claustrophobic. To her, a child makes demands merely by existing—and it has a right to a mother's undivided attention on a regular basis" (Safer, p. 85). The men's take on paternal responsibility was social, not personal. It wasn't that the needs of a child would overwhelm *them*, quite the contrary, but they as fathers couldn't prevent children from falling prey to unhealthy social pressures.

ALAN, 51, ELEMENTARY SCHOOL LIBRARIAN

Alan has been married 23 years to Shelly, also 51. She is a junior high school language arts teacher and they live in Eastern Washington. Alan's extensive education includes a master's degree, and ten to twelve classes a year for personal interest. His family was solid middle-class and nominally Presbyterian.

Tell me about the decision.

I was a student at National Taiwan University from 1969 through 1971 and I lived in Taipei. Every single day I was aware of the anthill, this area that had been destroyed by masses of human beings. I came back to the USA on a ship and it was the first time in 3 years that I had peace and quiet. I'm not sure today if that was the basis of my decision, because I had been religious about using birth control ever since I became sexually active in my late teens. Early on it was the fear of unwanted pregnancy, but after Taiwan the population issue came into it. I had a vasectomy in 1972.

When I met Shelly in 1973 and told her about it, she wondered only how her mother, who wanted grandchildren, would respond. Then we were interviewed in 1974 by someone doing doctoral research following up on men who had had vasectomies. We'd been married a year and the woman came to our house. We started talking and Shelly said, "If I had met a man who wanted children, I would have had children. But having met Alan, who didn't want children, I'm comfortable not having them. Sometimes, though, I wonder about the future," and then she burst into tears and ran upstairs. That was hard for me, because I had foreclosed that decision for Shelly.

Another influence was my sister who became pregnant as a freshman in college, had a shotgun wedding, was married for 17 years, and raised three children with no help from her husband. My father told me in no uncertain terms not to let any woman trap me into marriage, so I was very careful about birth control when I became sexually active.

My dad's been a profound influence in my life. He was a typical breadwinner, my mom a typical homemaker. Mom raised us, she did everything, she was the disciplinarian. But my father was always there, and we were a nuclear family that spent weekends together. I certainly have inherited my work ethics from him. Shelly remarks all the time that I am a chip off the old block.

You've said that freedom is most important to you. Why?

I just read Toni Morrison's novel, *Beloved*. My favorite line is Baby Suggs saying, "I couldn't understand why my son wanted to buy my freedom until I got to Ohio and realized that when I get up in the morning, I get to decide what to do." Children are shackles, the albatross around the neck. One of the reasons Shelly and I are saying "thank heaven" at this age is that all our peers are scrambling for college tuition. Since her mid-thirties Shelly has spent a lot traveling, but my money just piles up and it feels wonderful. I've never had a dependent in my life and I don't want one. I can imagine that in our old age, one of us will be a caregiver for the other, but that will be it.

You don't go traveling with Shelly?

I usually don't. I always say I can't afford it. We've had separate finances our whole married life. Shelly might suggest that we go to Papua, New Guinea. And I'd tell her that I can't afford it. She accuses me of gamesmanship because what happens is, she then buys plane tickets for both of us, and I go with her and only share the cost of lodging.

I travel a lot domestically. I spent July in Yellowstone while she was in England. I like to walk in wild places. I'm planning to spend every July for the rest of my life in Yellowstone where I can walk for a week and see only two other people. It's population-related, trying to find a haven with quiet.

You've also said that you've never felt a need to have children.

No. I'm trying to live as simple a life as possible, a Quaker lifestyle, grains and legumes. We are as vegetarian as we can be without being vegetarian. Shelly read a wonderful book called *Love What You Have*. The premise is that the relentless desire for more causes us to be unhappy and dissatisfied. Shelly and I live in a two-story, three-bedroom house. Two people. We justify it by saying it's an investment. So the cabin in the woods is part of the simple life.

How important is your career?

Not very. If I never went to my school again, I would miss it, but not much. I like elementary age kids. They are so sweet. We really are surrogate parents for kindergarteners and first graders. I don't know how Shelly teaches junior high. She's Joan of Arc to me.

If I'd stayed in the Air Force I'd have been eligible for 20-year retirement in 1984, 30-year retirement in 1994, but I've never regretted that I decided to get out and continue my education. And now we *could* retire. We own eight rental houses. At one time I thought, this is so much fun, maybe I'll do a hundred. I like doing the legwork and maintenance, finding tenants. I also have as much fun with money-management software as teenagers have with Nintendo. It cranks out net worth statements instantaneously. Whenever there's a significant change, I write the old figure and the new figure for Shelly and date it and leave it on the kitchen table where we pass notes to one another.

When I started teaching at age 40, I planned to retire at 50, and I would be retired now if I weren't married. Shelly isn't ready. I show her these net worth statements and she says, "That's great," but when I say, "Let's retire," she says, "What will we live on?" I say, "I just showed you that we can live comfortably for the rest of our lives on what we have right now." But Shelly wants to wait until the year 2000 when she'll be 55 with 25 years teaching and can start collecting her retirement check. She wants a check coming in, always.

Tell me why the idea of having time on your side is important.

I don't have enough of it in my life to do the things I want. That's why I would be retired now if I were a single person. I could be in Yellowstone 12 months out of the year. Shelly probably not. Her summer vacation was Britain and writing. If someone asks her what she does on a form, she writes "Writer/Educator." Teaching's not her self-identity. Our retirement plans are wide-open, but we both have a strong interest in the Hispanic countries and in birds. So we may spend our winters in South America.

I can see why a relationship played no part in your decision, but talk a little about it.

I was really committed to be childfree when I was single and 25 so my decision has nothing to do with my subsequent partnership. The greatest concession I ever made to Shelly's doubts about remaining childfree was that I once said I would give being a father a try. But I couldn't commit to raising a child, and if it didn't work out for me, then we wouldn't be partners anymore. I would leave, or she could leave, if she felt I wasn't the kind of father she wanted for her child.

Alan was not alone in watching his sister become a mother under difficult circumstances. So mom and dad are not the only family members who influence a man's decision. How a child impacts your sister's life—education, career, interests, personality—provides a short, sharp course in family living.

The key to early retirement for these three men, and several others motivated not to have kids so they could retire early, was not workaholism, but simply investing in real estate, frugal living, and saving. The workaholics—men who want as much time as possible for their careers—would go on working the rest of their lives if they could, and will retire only when forced to. Both types—in fact, almost all of the men—were long-range planners. It's a distinguishing characteristic of the childfree to think through the consequences of their actions and work toward specific goals.

As a last comment on early retirement, we might think that in retirement differences between parents and nonparents would fade, that empty-nesters, for example, would travel to their hearts' content, but maybe not. Here is what Glenn, early retired 61-year-old academic economist married 30 years to Ann, also 61, had to say about his travel and that of his good friend George, another early retired academic, and his wife Ruth.

Our being childfree meant when we were younger, we chose activities without regard to whether they would get in the way of time that was needed to be spent with children. We went to Europe often, went away lots of weekends, did a lot of physical activities, ran, swam, skiied, and bicycled, which it wouldn't have occurred to George and Ruth to do. Before retirement Ann and I got to looking at our home as wherever we wanted to be, rather than home as some fixed thing. George and Ruth were clearly tied to their home. Entertaining at home made it easier to accommodate children. Now, even though they're retired and the children are gone, living someplace else is a fearful thing. Their travel is determined by their kids. They stay in Portland because their son is there. When they go away, they go where their daughter is, never someplace new. Their children are continuing pushes or holds on their behavior.

Chapter 9

Avoiding Stress

Psychologists call it "role strain"—the difficulty of juggling work and family commitments without snapping in two. Back in the Eighties "juggling" was cast exclusively as a women's problem. But now, as more and more mothers go back to work, and more fathers take on an active parenting role while at the same time working ever longer hours, men are said to be suffering from role strain too. If confirmation were needed, this week European Commission figures showed that Britons work the longest hours in Europe. (David Cohen, 1996, p. 2)

ROLE STRAIN

David Cohen (1996) says that a survey of 1,100 managers found that 83% of men complained that on-the-job stress was hurting their family relationships, and 61% argued for more time with family and friends. He cites another survey in which 85% of men said that fathers should be *very involved in bringing their children up from an early age*. Small wonder Cohen concludes that the "image of the male hero has shifted from the one-track, risk-all, work-driven entrepreneur of the Eighties to something more fuzzy and undefined but which incorporates some concept of role diversity" (p. 3).

Avoiding stress by not having children came up repeatedly in the interviews I did prior to interviewing these men. For Carlo, the maintenance mechanic in Chapter 1 who had suffered 6- and 7-day workweeks and the threat of being laid off, keeping stress low has become a major life goal. For Sven, sailing instructor and househusband, periods of quiet reorganization are a must, not solely because he is used to solitude as an only child, but because Anna typically returns from work stressed-out. For Sid, the truck driver who developed ulcerative colitis, moving to a rural area has controlled the pressures in his life. Stress came up frequently in my subsequent interviews, although not necessarily under direct questioning.

Stress, like money worries or failing as a parent, is something men are loath to own up to on surveys and exercises. But when they talked about other issues, there it was. Finding your career at a low ebb is frustrating. Finding your career demanding the hell out of you is nerve-wracking. Finding your career is boring when you'd rather be an artist is depressing. They relieved their stress by building models and rebuilding engines, white-water kayaking, keeping a punchbag in the corner, and sailing off alone into the sunset.

MICHAEL, 53, PSYCHOLOGY PROFESSOR

Michael is a divorced social psychologist who teaches at a state-supported, 4-year college in central New Jersey. Michael's parents were both born into desperately poor, working-class families, but both nonetheless graduated from college. His father was Jewish and his mother a Catholic who converted to Judaism after Michael and his sister were born.

Tell me about your decision.

When I asked Corinne to marry me, I did the romantic, conventional thing and wrote my parents that I had met the woman of my dreams and I wanted her to be the mother of my children. In fact, I had no plan to have children, it was just the thing to say. Then I learned Corinne was frightened of childbirth and saw what a low threshold for irritability she had with her nieces and nephews.

So within 4 years we reached consensus about a decision we didn't even talk about. I went to have a vasectomy but balked when he started talking about auto-immune reactions to sperm and backed off. To fast forward, I had the vasectomy in 1986 after I had been divorced several years. It felt like something I was intending to do all along and I should finally do.

Did you tell your parents about your decision?

No, my mother brought the topic up only once. We got married in July and the following Mother's Day we called her to say Happy Mother's Day and the first thing out of her mouth was, "Well, maybe you'll be calling me in a year to tell me I'm a grandmother." We changed the subject and it never came up again.

*You've indicated strongly that you are not interested
in child-centered activities.*

I'm only interested in children as creatures whose minds I want to know as a psychologist. I don't want to go to the zoo with kids and not be able to think about ethology and primatology, but have to be concerned about how some 5-year-old is experiencing a chimpanzee.

In the mid-seventies my sister decided to have a baby. She is the person I most love in the world. I was fascinated at what she was doing because it was so different from what I wanted. I began reading the technical literature on childbearing and constructed an interdisciplinary course in which I taught the anthropology, biology, midwifery, medicine, and psychology of childbearing. I got to know the whole obstetrical underground, the midwives and doctors who were practicing illegally. I studied birth defects in detail and learned that their probability is much higher than I thought it would be. Although my sister has had three healthy, normal children, she had no idea what she might have gotten herself into.

Perhaps somewhere in a parallel universe there is a Michael who had children and is a very good father who has wonderful relationships with them, even as teenagers, and who has grown in ways that I never will. But in other parallel universes, there is a Michael who is desperately unhappy with how his kids turned out and he is still married to the same turkey of a wife for the sake of the kids and he thinks of his life as a disaster. I never wanted to become that person.

I don't want to be overwhelmed. My women friends have often commented on this, that I'm perfectly willing to take full responsibility for my students. I do lots of extracurricular nurturing and tutoring. But when the day ends, I want to come home to peace and quiet and my two formerly stray cats.

You've said, and it's a rare thing, that you could have been disappointed in rearing children.

Some of my disillusionment comes from reading the *New York Times*. Most crime is committed by juvenile males and I think about the pain in their parents' lives. The *Times* interviews the mother who talks about what a cute little boy he was 8 years ago and now he's a murderer and a rapist and a drug dealer. Then I have seen how much pain my friend Evelyn has suffered when her kids disappointed her. One became a habitual liar as a teenager and the other upset her by dropping out of college and joining the navy. As a teenager I also caused my father a lot of pain. I was perfectly nice, normal, and decent, the teacher's pet, and yet for reasons I don't understand, I stopped making eye contact with him and stopped sharing things with him. He became loathsome in my eyes. That dear, wonderful man did not deserve anything like the treatment I accorded him when I was a teenager. And, unfortunately, he died before I was mature enough for reconciliation.

You've said you are very happy as you are. How is that?

Fulfillment to me is Alfred Adler's work and love and friendship. Find the right kind of work, the right place to do it, and do it with zest. As for love, I have enjoyed a succession of monogamous relationships since my marriage. For 3 years I lived with Evelyn, whose ex-husband had custody of the children. Having the children with us every other weekend was the biggest mistake of my life. An important value of mine is to avoid anger. Evelyn was repeatedly angered by her son and daughter and I saw a side of her I had never seen when we were just friends. She confessed that if she had her life to do over, she would erase her son from it.

Interestingly, you are not as concerned about freedom as many men are.

I'm not a sensation-seeking person. I simply want to avoid disasters, as opposed to maximizing benefits. I know the style of life I want to pursue for the rest of life. I'm going to be teaching at the same college for another 15 years, living in the same house where I now live, staying close to my sister in Brooklyn, reading the *New York Times* every day, and, I hope, contributing something of enduring value to my students and civilization. If I could, I'd also see my mother every day. When she first moved here from the West Coast she moved to an apartment three blocks from me. When her savings ran out, my sister found an apartment near her in Brooklyn where she was eligible for Section 8 housing support.

What I'm most looking forward to now is the next woman in my life. It's been 8 months since I resigned from my relationship with Samantha and I'm missing female company. This woman has to be totally childfree. She can't even have grown children, because grown children bring the threat of grandchildren and babysitting.

Kathleen Gerson (1993) said of the New York City childfree men she studied: "One way to offset or reduce the potential isolation of avoiding parenthood is to find a special partner . . . and most of the single men hoped to find an ongoing relationship. But, consciously or unconsciously, they chose or searched for partners who would provide companionship without pushing for children, thus promising them the greatest amount of freedom" (p. 199). As Michael illustrates, special partners can prove illusive.

THOMAS, 27, HOTEL MARKETING DIRECTOR

Thomas, single, works for a small, exclusive Portland hotel. He grew up in St. Louis, Missouri with his divorced father and younger sisters. His family was middle-class and nondenominational. He has a bachelor's degree in marketing. Thomas showed me a folder of information on no scalpel vasectomy (NSV), which he was planning the next winter when it would interfere least with his sports activities.

Tell me about your decision and how others have reacted to it.

It dates from when I broke up with my last girlfriend 2 years ago over the child issue. Up until I was 19 I thought it was part of your life to raise kids. When I reached 20, I started paying attention to lifestyles and started the educational process of, "Is this something I really want to do?" By the time I got out of college, I knew that children were not going to be a good fit for me.

I went with Kate for 5 years, and after I got settled in Portland, she joined me. Then I finally announced that I knew for certain I had no interest in raising children. And she said, "Well, I really want kids and I expect you to play a large role in raising them." It reached a point where it was a major stumbling block that we were never going to get over.

I haven't seen a whole lot of model families that I would look at and say, "That's a great family and I'd like to bring up my kids like that." In the environment I grew up in, from grade school on, parents were divorced, siblings bickered, some kids turned out so-so. My parents divorced when I was in the first grade, and I was responsible for raising my sisters. We stayed with my dad and spent summers with my mom.

I've talked to my mom about it but not my dad. I broke off contact with him in college. Neither of my sisters wants to have kids either, so my mom says it's up to me. She thinks I'd make a wonderful parent. She keeps saying, "Please don't do anything permanent." I tell her, "Hey, Mom, it's my life."

Is your decision connected to your relationship with your father?

Definitely. My parents' divorce was a major life event. Then I had to take care of my sisters, taking them with me everywhere, being home if they had to be home and my dad wasn't home. I cooked, did laundry, picked up, and as a result I do very well living alone. My dad put a lot of responsibility on me from fifth grade on. He started taking Fridays off work because he said he wanted to spend more time with us, which was real weird because we were in school til 3:00. He really wanted to spend time with his car.

You've said that having enough time for all the things you're into is paramount.

I've always been very involved in extracurricular activities. I don't expect them to stay the same for the rest of my life, but whether it's photography, camping, or bonsai, there'll be things I want to pursue. Right now it's volleyball, mountain biking, and water polo. I'm president of a local mountain biking club. I help organize sports tournaments for various causes, like a bike ride for the American Lung Association, or a volleyball tournament to benefit United Way. I also coach college kids and younger kids. I also want time to further my education, read books, take classes. The last class I took was on oriental interior design, feng shui, that I thought would develop another skill useful in the hotel business.

Ever since I was in high school I've needed my own space and my own time, whether it's at home or in a relationship, every day. I need to sit back, focus, set my priorities. I can do it when I'm working out, or stretching. I get away daily for at least a half hour to take a walk.

You've also indicated that avoiding stress is one of your goals. Tell me about it.

I do not have the patience to raise kids. I learned that raising a dog. I'd hit my dog when I shouldn't have. I have two cats. Same thing, if they get on my nerves, I've hit them. If you have kids, you can't do that. Coaching water polo, I've said things that have hurt the kids and that's all because of lack of patience. After about a half hour, it's like, "Get me out of the room." They're loud, they're undisciplined, they're beating on my nerves. I have no control over them. You put an infant next to me and I have no desire to pick it up.

This summer I'm coaching 10 and unders and it's brutal, fifteen kids in a pool. The testosterone or whatever it is that makes these boys fly is going a 100 miles an hour. I almost quit after the first night. People keep telling me that raising kids is such a great learning experience, but I've learned about it these other ways. Take discipline. You need to be real careful about what you say, and I've always said whatever is at the top of my head. Then they'll pick on one word and boom, they're mad at me for the rest of the season.

I've got high blood pressure. If I ended up having children, I would take on the responsibility the same way I take on everything else. I tend to be a Type A personality, walking on the razor's edge, and once you step over, you've lost it. Kids would put me over.

You mentioned a dog and cats, so pets must be important to you.

They are. I had to put my dog to sleep. It was an awful experience because he completely relied on me for food, nurturing, and loving. He was 13, old and sick and he couldn't move around, but he had lived with me during those developmental years and meant a lot to me. I blubbered like a baby. I decided after that I didn't want to have another dog. Cats are independent and I can leave them with food and water and go away for the weekend. You can't do that with a dog, or a baby. These two cats were strays and headed for the pound. I tend to do that, pick up responsibilities.

You've said that a satisfying relationship is one of your motives.

I don't want my relationship spoiled by my partner taking on the role of a mother. I've had three serious relationships and communication was a problem in all of them. Kids mean a third variable. Maybe if my parents hadn't had kids and spent time fixing their problems, they would have stayed together. I looked at them and decided, "That's not going to happen to me."

I want somebody to make *me* happy. If I had a kid, the attention's going to go to that kid. I don't want to compete with some kid. My latest strategy for finding a partner is to recognize that if I don't have those feelings that have worked for me in other relationships, I drop her right away. In the past I would have dated that person until I found somebody new, but now, if on a first date, she mentions she wants kids, the date for me is over. I figure I'll be 30 before I start finding people. Once women reach 30, they may not want kids to interfere with their careers, or they've developed routines that they want to continue.

Why are you least concerned about being in control of your life?

Simple. My planning for the future is pretty much week by week.

Then the issue of leaving a legacy to children isn't an issue for you at all.

It comes up a lot. I'm passing things on in a lot of ways. I can be an important asset to my community with my coaching, volunteering for community activities, donating 5% of my money to nonprofit groups that I think are doing great work. If you have a kid, what's going to go first? Charitable donations and time.

How important is your career to you?

When I got out of school, I was definitely fast track, Fortune 500 company, move up the ladder, bounce around from place to place. But after my first job I realized I like having a home base. You can make a lot of money in a job and hate your life. I may not get as wealthy as I would someplace else, but it's not as stressful. I've been here for 3 years and my boss, the owner, is a great guy. I could easily work for him for a long time, the way he's treated me. Forty-hour week. You need time off, you take it. He gives all of his employees who work more than 32 hours a week health insurance, which is unheard of in the hotel/restaurant industry. This job means a lot to me.

Fortunately, Thomas has insight into his condition. "Type A men are as much plagued by others' shortcomings as by their own. Their impatience and competitiveness combine with perfectionism to drive them to perform, perform, perform . . . . Being the child or wife of a Type A man is as difficult as being the Type A man himself" (Witkin-Lanoil, 1986, p. 47). As Thomas says, he doesn't want to compete with a kid; if he's his partner's one-and-only, he'll be far less difficult to live with.

NATHAN, 32, DULCIMER PLAYER

Nathan fled Iran in 1985 because he did not want to fight in the war with Iraq and because of his Baha'i faith. Single, he lives in Wales and works part-time as a musician and supermarket sales assistant. His middle-class father, mother, and three sisters still live in Iran, where his father is an engineer.

Tell me about your decision and how your family has reacted to it.

In my family in Iran, I have lots of cousins and everybody was always getting pregnant and I saw these children grow up and with my own eyes saw the wrong things that their parents did. These parents knew nothing about childrearing, so they were wasting their time and their children were suffering. They were not prepared to raise children and I have never felt ready.

The government let my mother come here last year for 9 months. While she was here we discussed my wish not to have children. She pointed out all the good things about having them, but in the end she said, "We don't want to force you, but we would prefer it." Because in Iran, and especially in religious cultures, society expects you to have children, otherwise something's wrong with you. My family is more open-minded and liberated than most of Iranian society. So much so that my sisters are prisoners in their own home because they will not accept chauvinist, sexist men.

Unfortunately, they cannot come to the UK because the government won't let unmarried women leave. The Islamic Revolution says they would be spoiled by Western countries.

Why have you said that you don't want children because of the stress involved?

In the past I've been depressed, with lots of anxieties and phobias. I've overcome most of them and I'm going in a positive direction now. My two jobs help me, and the fact that I've started teaching the dulcimer. But my soul has scars on it. I couldn't stand worrying about children, and I can do more positive things in life than raise them. Most important to me is that my home is calm and relaxed without noise and destruction. Also, raising a normal, healthy child is a struggle. With a child disabled at birth you are doing a double job to cope with that person. I couldn't manage that.

Mostly because of my shyness, I've never had a girlfriend. I want to find a lady friend and share the rest of my life with her, but not have children. When the Revolution happened, I was age 15. From that point on, we weren't allowed to have girlfriends and boyfriends. The situation was so bad that if a brother and sister were walking down the street, they were hounded, "Are you married? Are you married?" Now marriages are arranged by parents, and most couples don't even know each other.

Personal development is very important to you. Explain, please.

I've always been interested in developing myself. That's how I've managed to overcome my problems. Every day I get a little better. Eight years ago I became very anxious and didn't want to socialize anymore. I was afraid to travel. I knew I needed help. I went to a community therapy center and got counseling. They gave me relaxation tapes and taught me breathing techniques because I had fainted a few times in meetings and didn't know the reason. It was hyperventilation.

The other thing I've done is read psychology books and come to realize the mistakes my parents made. They are loving people, but if you spoil your children, they will have problems. My parents were overprotective. "Don't do that. Don't do this. No. No. That's dangerous." They wanted me to go to university and because Britain did not accept my high school diploma, I tried and failed A-level exams in biology, maths, and chemistry. I was just doing what my parents wanted. Some of my problems go back to them, others go back to the Revolution.

In my letters to my parents I have explained to them what they did wrong. They accept that they may have done *some* things wrong, but they emphasize all the good things they provided. They think they were right and that *I* have to do something about my problems myself. I agree, and I'm doing my best.

I also do not want to give up the time I now devote to my music. I play a traditional instrument called a dulcimer, or santoor in Persian. My parents recognized when I was a child that I had a talent for music, but they didn't let me go for it. They wanted me to be a doctor. Islamic society doesn't appreciate music. But it wasn't until I talked about escaping that my parents relented, and as a last resort to get me to stay my father finally said I could study music. I had a private teacher for 6 months and I continued after I left Iran, learning the notes and the principles. After 3 years of practicing in England, I also learned tuning, which is the most difficult part. At the moment, there are three of us playing at a Persian restaurant. One guy plays the keyboard and the other plays Persian drums and sings. It's in my blood now, I could play all the time. I'm now teaching the santoor 2 hours a week.

You've said that being free of routines is very important.

Yes. Children mean routine. I want to have new experiences with just the right woman. But I have a fear of rejection. I cannot convince myself yet to ask a girl to go have a drink because I'm afraid she'll say no. When I was a teenager I was in love with several girls, but I never told them because you couldn't in that situation. Then when I escaped to Pakistan with some cousins, I fell in love with one of the girls. I didn't know how to express my feelings. Perhaps I tried to help her too much. Maybe she suspected I wanted sex or had some ulterior motive. She became very nasty toward me, which I had a hard time getting over.

I'm from the middle class, but when middle-class girls see me in the store working as a sales assistant, they think I am less than them. The money I make is working-class money. I'm not in the right place to show myself, and the women I meet don't know what my potential is. I need to get into some new activities where I can meet a girl who will understand how I am and someone who doesn't care how much money I make.

*Was your decision related in any way to your relationship
with your father?*

He never talked seriously with me. When there were guests in the house, if somebody asked me something, my parents would jump in and say, "No, Nathan doesn't like that, Nathan likes this. When Nathan was a child, he did this, he did that." They didn't let me talk as an adult. So he has a lot to do with my lack of confidence.

How about the issue of who will take care of you when you're old?

I'm not worried about myself, but I am about my parents. In Western countries there are places where old people go to stay and old age is not a problem. In my country old people have to live with their relatives, usually their children. It concerns me because I don't want to ever go back. I will suggest that my parents come here to live, and maybe they'll accept if my father loses his job. It would be very hard on them to leave. In my country everybody knows everybody else, so to come here they would be very homesick.

I think a very important subpopulation of men around the globe who should seriously consider whether they could be good fathers are men from war-torn countries. If a man's developmental years have been stressed by revolution, violence, and killing, perhaps there are scars on some souls out there that need to be attended to more than trying to raise children.

DOUG, 47, MAINFRAME COMPUTER OPERATOR

Doug, single, lives in Tacoma, Washington. He has two bachelor's degrees in business administration and in sociology. He is the youngest child from a middle-class, Protestant family in which his father was an engineer and mother a school teacher. Doug had a vasectomy at age 30.

Tell me about your decision.

There were four kids in our family and our next-door neighbors had six, and all I saw was continual strife and squabbling going on between kids and parents. As a kid I couldn't imagine spending money this way when you could be off flying airplanes or sailing a boat across the ocean. When I was 7 years old we were driving to the store and I asked, "Mom, what's the purpose of having kids?" And she said, "Well, to have kids." And I said, "What's the purpose of them having kids?" I couldn't articulate it at the time, but I was thinking, "Okay, who ultimately does the living that makes it all worthwhile?" Our conversation also revealed to me that her purpose in life *was* to have kids. That's true today, because the family is the center of my parents' life, raising responsible children and sending them off to college.

My folks didn't drink, didn't smoke, great parents from an outsider's point of view. They are pretty much on the same wave-length when it comes to children, spending money, values. They're still married, for 55 years now. To me, though, they were oppressive because they placed so much emphasis on studying and excelling. All of us have at least 5 years of college, two of my sibs have master's degrees.

You are unusual in that what you want time for is not your job but community work.

Yes, the group I've been most involved in is Common Cause, it's nonpartisan, nonprofit, all the money comes from membership. Here in Washington State we have over 6,000 members and I've been in a leadership position since 1982. I'm also a member of organizations like Planned Parenthood that I contribute money to on a regular basis. And my will says I'm giving all my money away to good charities.

I was very proud when Common Cause forced the hand of the opposition in 1992, so that they put an initative on the ballot, Initiative 134, that was passed by the voters and limits contributions to politicians. Also, we were one of the primary promoters of the redistricting commission.

A job is a means to provide a comfortable living and I'm not picky as long as it's a pleasant environment. I want to work among nice people, not have too much overtime, and not take the job home with me. My personal peace of mind is what's important. Up until the age of 27 I felt like I was in a pressure cooker and I don't want to do that anymore.

One often-heard sentiment is, "I'm going to raise kids who will make the world a better place." I suggest to these people, "Why don't you go out and do those good things yourself and don't worry about the kids? If you don't have kids, you'll have the time and the means."

You're trying to live a stress-free lifestyle?

You bet. In college I had to work part-time, so that cut down on my hours for studying. Then right out of college I was drafted into the Air Force. I went in as an officer, became a pilot, and ended up flying the aircraft of my dreams, a C-141 Starlifter, a large transport-type airplane bigger than most airliners. I flew mostly overseas routes to Europe and the Orient. I wouldn't know from day to day if I was leaving the country the next day. I'd call between 3:00 and 5:00 in the afternoon and they might say, "Nothing's going on," or they might say, "You're going to Japan tomorrow. Be here at 5:00." I couldn't plan my life, and it was a life-or-death job, so I was constantly studying to be up to it. I was also very uncomfortable to be part of the military establishment while the U.S. government was involved in an immoral war overseas.

I got out of the Air Force in 1976 under an early-out program, and that's when the cork was unpopped and I was allowed to depressurize. For the first time in my life I was able to do what I wanted, when I wanted, and where I wanted. I packed up everything and went to a small town in Eastern Washington, and went back to college. I wanted a small town and a college that wasn't too big or too small. I lived there for 6 years on my investments, had lots of time for reading and activities.

I also want the freedom to change jobs. In 1987, I was working a lot of unpaid overtime and I just up and quit. I haven't always done computer programmer jobs, I've done other things, like technical writing. I'd like to get back to writing.

Why is personal freedom so important to you?

So I can travel whenever I want to. I went to Australia last October. I've been to Europe a number of times and I go on a lot of ski trips—weekends, 4-day trips, a full week at some resort. One reason I rent this apartment is I want to be able to take off and ski when I want. I don't have to fix anything, it's maintenance-free.

When I go abroad I stake myself out in a city, see what there is to see, and then do daytrips out into the countryside. My favorite was Amsterdam, but I've also done this in Bonn, Sydney, London, Washington, DC.

You've indicated that your decision had the least to do with wanting to preserve a relationship.

Right. I don't have a partner so all those issues don't apply.

Everybody knows that in general married men are happier and healthier than single men. Certainly as far as job stress is concerned, the married men here were doing better than the single men. Kazuo, an engineer from Japan, Gordon, the Microsoft programmer, Frank, the systems analyst, and Roger who sells wood products to Japan, have tremendous job stress ameliorated by marriages to homemakers.

One in five women out there today does not want a child. They're waiting to be found on college campuses, among hotel clients and restaurant customers, and at meetings of activist causes. But what's stress-reducing for the majority, may be stress-inducing for a minority. Was it an accident that the four men featured in this chapter turned out to be single? Maybe not. Maybe for some men staying single is another way to avoid stress.

Georgia Witkin-Lanoil (1986) who does therapy with stressed-out men says, unfortunately, single men get more stressed by the passage of time:

First, they become increasingly aware that they may themselves be contributing to their single state. That is, the older man is less likely to say that he has not yet found the right woman, and more likely to ask himself if he could deal with her if he did. . . . Second, men who have not married and are approaching their middle years speak of the fear of being alone. Although most are not lonely, they worry that they may become . . . no longer able to date, and, finally, isolated. (p. 171)

Chapter 10

Staying the Way We Are

> Childless adults have always come under close scrutiny from parents in our society who cannot imagine any other way of life. But nonparenting adults are very much like anyone else. They enjoy happy marriages, they buy homes, they care about their neighborhoods and communities. They enjoy the traditions of the holidays, contribute their time and money to charities, work hard at their careers. (Leslie Lafayette, 1995, p. 76)

Consider the following quote. "Once a woman faces her personality and her past and makes the decision not to have a child, she confronts another equally daunting task: on what is she going to base her identity as a woman and as a person now that she has renounced the traditional defining role? What is her relation to a society of parents and families? What will give her life meaning?" (Safer, 1996, p. 143).

Could this be said of men? From what I learned in this project, I'd have to say "no," unequivocally—these words do not apply to childfree men. No such daunting task faces voluntarily childless men. They settle comfortably into the identities they already have, relieved of the necessity to change their personalities to be more patient, child-centered, and conservative about career change. The men were happy as they were and they felt no need to have children. In fact, holding on to the identities they'd already forged was a popular motive for remaining childless, whereas Jeanne Safer says a woman who chooses not to be a mother must forge an alternative feminine identity.

To illustrate what about their identities they didn't want to change, we'll start with Jerry.

JERRY, 42, NEWSPAPER ARTIST

Jerry works for a San Francisco newspaper. He is single, from a middle-class Jewish family living in Los Angeles, and has a longstanding relationship with Lydia that may lead to marriage but won't lead to children.

Tell me about your decision and how others have reacted to it.

I was a difficult child, and every so often I'd get this line, "Wait til you have kids. All the grief we're having, you'll have to deal with it. The same headaches." So at age 10, I had the idea, "No, I won't."

When I brought it up with my parents, like, "Gee, I don't know if I want to go through this," my mom changed the subject and I never brought it up again. My dad said, "Well, your mother and I decided we wanted to have kids and this was our choice and we're very happy with the choice, but it's your life." My mom's passive, my dad's very dynamic, so the push-pull in my life has been with my father.

I didn't have my first date until I was 20 and these early relationships didn't get to the point where we talked about marriage. Then I had two really significant relationships. One, with Betsy, lasted 3 years. I loved this woman very much, she loved me, emotionally we had this very strong bond, but there were all these compatibility problems, like she clearly wanted kids. Maybe 15% of me was open to the idea. That was the only time I even came close.

After that I decided to go through personal ads, and in my ad the very first thing I mentioned was that I didn't want kids. I found a half dozen women to date from that ad. One was Lydia, who's been on and off in my life since 1990. We broke up in 1994 because she wanted to get married and I wasn't ready to. After we broke up I placed another personal ad and got eight responses and Lydia was one of them. She figured there was an 80% likelihood it was me.

Not having to be grown up all the time appeals to you. Why?

I have a definite sense of wanting to be a child. Part of my work is cartoons. That's about as childlike an activity as somebody can get paid for out there in the world. I'm the younger of two children. My sister had a lot more responsibility dumped on her as the older sibling. I was on the lazy side, I didn't want to work. That's the thing I grapple with in my life. Mostly I want to be a kid playing in the sun. A child would get in the way of being a child myself.

And part of not being grown up is being free to move around.

Yeah. I like to spontaneously decide to go out to dinner, see a movie, do day trips, take off for the weekend. We like to explore art museums, historic and science museums, and galleries. I like to look at the architecture of a city, to wander through the heart of urban centers. More important, I'd like to move back to L.A. to be closer to my family, Lydia's hesitation notwithstanding. Unfortunately, there are very few job openings in what I do. I've looked into jobs where I would have taken a considerable pay cut, but

I'd get to do more cartooning and less graphics and charts that are used on a daily basis by a newspaper. I'm willing to trade income for pleasure but so far it hasn't worked out.

You seem amused by the idea that you've chosen not to have children because you don't like them.

Because if you want to come across as an ogre, just say, "I don't like children." I like them in limited quantities, in limited times. But when I'm in a restaurant or shopping center and kids are throwing a tantrum, very quickly I feel myself getting less mellow and a sense of irritation creeping into my personality that I don't like. When I see a friend's child misbehaving, I feel myself getting angry, and I wonder if I were a parent if I'd start yelling.

Childrearing goes on well beyond 18 years. Kids don't leave home, they go off and have financial problems and come back. Or they do go off and have children and the cycle repeats. I could never cope with a child who had birth defects. I have an aunt who is mentally retarded and I can never relate to the woman.

Yet you're one of the many men who said they couldn't be disappointed with their children.

If I were childrearing, yes, I wouldn't want to be disappointed by my children. Were I in that position, I wouldn't be a perfectionist, but I'd certainly try to do a decent job.

Why do men get so little pressure from other men to have kids?

Because the average male could have 'em or he couldn't. His parents, co-workers, neighbors have kids, so he expects he'll have kids. A few men really want to be daddies, that's their big goal, and a few like me don't, but the average man goes with what his partner wants. You can imagine having fun with your son, like playing catch or going fishing, and you'll have somebody to carry on the family name, but you're also going to lose so much income and have so many headaches. The average man sees the pro and con, and it adds up to a neutral. Men are also neutral because they don't intend to co-parent, "No, I'm not going to get up for 3 a.m. feedings and I'm not going to change diapers." So when another man says "no" to kids, that's fine by them.

Leslie Lafayette (1995) agrees. "Men can afford to be more realistic, less idealistic, about parenthood because they have less of their own self-esteem invested in it than do women. Their role in life is not defined by parenthood. . . . Unlike women, they don't get left out in the cold if they don't have children" (p.139).

PAUL, 42, COMPANY VICE-PRESIDENT

Paul has degrees in wildlife biology and electronics engineering. He has risen to be vice-president of a Portland firm that designs and manufactures medical electronics. He is not married but has lived for

7 years with Meg, 33, who sells real estate. Paul grew up in Ohio in a Southern Baptist, Ozzie and Harriet, upper-middle class family and has two older brothers.

Tell me about your decision and your family's reaction to it.

I was a postponer, but there's never been the urge. Since my early twenties I've always put the cards on the table. I'm fairly strong-willed and it's been understood that it was not just, "No." It was, "Hell, no." In fact, there were two abortions, one in my twenties, one in my thirties, as a result of birth control failing, one IUD, one diaphragm. Basically my girlfriends have all been agreeable and there was never any discussion about, "Oh, wouldn't it be nice to have children?"

I'm not close to my family. My parents probably can guess what I've decided, but I've never made it a big deal. My parents are great. They're celebrating their fiftieth anniversary. They were the classic family, single breadwinner and mother stays home. They raised me with the sentiment that, "We don't care what you do, as long as you're happy doing it. You can be a ditchdigger as long as you're the best damned ditchdigger there is and you like doing it." So if I don't want to have kids, they will understand it.

You aren't interested in child-centered activities. Would you elaborate, please?

I'm not interested in circuses, playgrounds, Disneyland, Little League. I'm interested in wildlife photography, white-water kayaking, having a beer with folks, going on solo backpack trips. Unfortunately right now, I'm also an administrator dealing with the crisis of the day. I was a design engineer and worked my way up through the ranks. It was 30 people when we started and now it's 350. I have 10 project directors and 60 engineer-technicians reporting to me. That's a lot of people. Plus I've got customer issues to deal with, from billion-dollar-a-year corporate types to people starting up with barely any money.

My job's become dealing with people all day long and it's like having a bunch of children. The last thing I want to do is to go home and have to put on the happy face and be there for my child, because I think that is real important. A parent should be always able to listen and not be short. A parent must always make time for the child and be willing to go to Disneyland. They should like to go see PG13 movies and enjoy children at play. Otherwise your negative feelings are going to show up in the child, who is going to have problems. My guess is that if I suddenly did become a parent, I'd do okay. But it's not a choice I would make.

Tell me about the importance of freedom to you.

I have lots of freedom both at work and play. In my play I don't plan out things too far. I haven't traveled around the world much because that requires prior planning, and I wouldn't want to do it on a tight timetable. Lots of times I go on short photography trips by myself and I don't have an itinerary per se. If I want to go someplace different from what I first decided, I just do it.

I also have a lot of freedom at work. I report to the president, and he's a very hands-off individual. I have total freedom in how I manage people. That's why I've been there for 10 years. Up until then I'd never stayed anywhere longer than 2 years. The way things are, if I want to quit my job tomorrow, it would be scary, but I could. I don't have a mother-wife telling me to be home by such and such time, or that I can't kayak because of the risks. I'm going white-water kayaking next year in Costa Rica and then head for the southern part of Chile where there's a wildlife refuge I'd like to cruise through.

Did this strong sense of independence come from how you were raised?

I think so. In many ways I was raised as an only child because my brothers were much older. At 15, I worked in a restaurant downtown. To get to it I had to go through a section of town where there were taverns with people getting shot all the time. Nowadays I couldn't imagine sending a teenager into that neighborhood. My father worked very hard, moving from blue-collar work to being a white-collar executive. We never did a lot of the traditional father-son things together, like fishing. Weekends he worked on the house and the cars, and there was only the one-week-a-year family vacation. So in that way my upbringing was independent.

What do mean by wanting to preserve your identity?

What I dislike at work now, with the growth and complexity, is that my time is out of my control. I'm willing to accept it for the present because the payoff is there. Instead of being super happy right now, my identity is more a matter of *not* having major dissatisfactions. I don't wake up in the morning and think, "God, I wish I could quit this job, God, I wish I could leave this city." I contrast my situation with that of my oldest brother. He's got four children from two marriages. The two older are problems, they flunked out of college and haven't been traditionally successful. He's got two new kids and he's not satisfied with his job. There's the financial burden on him, the pressures are big and bad and he's trapped. He can't quit.

Why isn't maintaining a relationship important to you?

It comes down to my independence. I've never met anyone who was so essential that I wanted to do the marriage thing. The funny thing is that our household runs along pretty traditional lines. Meg defers to me on home location, car repair, all the stereotyped manly things, and she takes care of the meals and the laundry. I bought five acres with a standard house on it, no big yard, not a lot to take care of. I've got neighbors with noisy children who drive me nuts, come over on my property with their bb guns, which means eventually another move to more acreage and greater isolation. I have made a commitment to a dog. He's a little bit of a style cramper, but I can put him in his pen. You can't do that with children.

Jerry's identity rests in a job where he never has to be quite grown up. In contrast, Paul's identity rests in a job where he has to be very grown up—the father-figure administrator. Away from work, what they're drawn to are adult activities, Jerry's urban, Paul's back country. But neither is likely to encounter kids in their travels. They also share never having felt the need for children.

KAZUO, 33, MECHANICAL ENGINEER

Kazuo, from Japan, has been married 6 years to 42-year-old Melanie who is American and a housewife. They moved to Tacoma, Washington from Japan 3 years ago and live in an immaculate, white-carpeted, custom-built, large country home furnished with delicate Japanese antiques. Kazuo's family is middle-class and Buddhist.

Tell me about your decision and how your family reacted to it.

I always wanted to have children, because I like children and Melanie does too. But she had seen so many kids who have mental disorders, she was afraid she might have a child like that. Also pregnancy is more risky in older women than younger women. So I agreed with her that we'd have none.

We met at a party. I was taking an English class through my company in Tokyo. Our teacher from a nearby U.S. Air Force base held a party and invited Melanie and other American women who worked there. She was a speech pathologist and worked with students at the base school who had speech problems. It was when I asked her to marry me that she asked if I was interested in having children. I said yes and asked her if she did. She said, "Ah, well, not really." So we decided to get married and not have children at the same time.

I'm the oldest of three boys. The oldest child is very special in Japan. He always takes care of the parents and usually has the first grandchildren. My parents expected us to have children, and I didn't tell them about our decision before we were married. Afterward, they kept asking me. It was very difficult. Now that they have grandchildren it's easier. My brother's married and they have two children so my parents are satisfied. They used to insist, "Which one has the problem?" I would say, "No, there is no physical problem." And there wasn't at first, but a year after we were married Melanie had an ovarian cyst and had to have one ovary removed. From that point on my parents accepted our decision.

You've said that you don't like what children do to their parents' personalities.

I don't like to see parents yelling at children. I don't like to listen to people who talk about nothing but their kids, their schools, sports, constantly. I don't want to be someone like that, with kids always occupying your head, not able to think or talk about anything else. When I visited my brother's children back in Japan, my nieces, they're lovely little girls, a 2-year-old and a 1-year-old, they are the center of attention, toys are scattered all over the place, and they demand their mother's attention every minute. Even though they're wonderful children, after 5 minutes with them, it's enough. I feel sorry for my brother. Motorcycles used to be his hobby but no more. He's told me he wishes he could get away sometimes from the family, to have time for a hobby or just to have his private, quiet time. I don't want that to happen to me.

*Did Melanie share your fears of what happens to people
when they become parents?*

Japan is very traditional and women have the whole responsibility for raising children. The mother is totally in charge of educating the children and any kind of misbehavior is always blamed on mothers. That's what she was afraid of, that I was going to give all the responsibility to her. She didn't think that I would take care of them too. But I would have.

You've said that you spend a lot of time at your job. Tell me about it.

My job is very, very important to me. I'm an engineer but I'm now responsible for customer service, product support, marketing, and sales. I do a lot of overtime. I've been with the company 11 years. To be honest, I don't want to go back to Japan if the company asks me to. So I need to be even more flexible, because if the company tells us to go back, I'll leave them. Ideally, I'd like to start my own business. I've dedicated myself to them but they don't give me anything extra for it. A typist who has worked for the company for 30 years makes more money than I do.

This makes me feel very insecure. I've never changed jobs. If you change companies in Japan, you start at the bottom. But there are many opportunities in the U.S. and here my experience will count for something with a new company. There's also the possibility that they'll open another office in the eastern U.S. So, all the time I feel, "When's this going to happen?" I'm glad that I don't have to think about, "What are we going to do about the children?"

What else do you want time for?

Recreation. Since we moved here, we bought a computer and I've learned how to use it. We have different kinds of computers in Japan. We have a big yard, an acre, and I enjoy gardening. We grow a lot of flowers in containers. I go to an exercising club and I've started to play golf. I spend a lot of time on home furnishings, restoring Japanese antique furniture. I did the tea tansu in that corner and the small writing desk in this corner and that hibachi.

I like our two dogs a lot. Just taking care of them, petting them, watching them play. We looked for over 6 months to find the right dogs. We travel a lot so we had to get two so that they have each other's company at the kennel. These two are brother and sister and were abandoned in a rest area on the highway. They were a year old when we adopted them.

You've said you couldn't have been disappointed with your children?

If I had children, my children would be wonderful. I would spend a lot of time with them. Time spent with them would be more important than time at my job. What's most important is each child's special talent. Athletics, art, mathematics, language skills. Every child has his own potential skill. I wouldn't judge my kids. I would bring their special talents out. I couldn't be disappointed.

It's very important in Japan that a man have children. Japanese people think first, that if men and women don't get married, they're not stable. Second, if they are married and they don't have children, perfect strangers will ask, "Why? What's wrong with you? Is it physical, mental, or emotional?" The biggest question is, "Who's going to take care of the family name for the next generation?"

Companies think that couples with children are more responsible. Until recently, it was hard for single people to get promoted. That's why we still have arranged marriages, so that if you get to a certain age and haven't been promoted, you can marry quickly. If I'd been single, they'd never have sent me to the U.S. Always I'm asked by people at work, "When are you going to have children?"

Is overpopulation an issue in Japan?

No. Our biggest concern is that medical technology is producing more senior age people than the younger generations. Japan is concerned about how they are going to support the elderly in the future, not global overpopulation. I'm not the kind of person who chose not to have children because of overpopulation in the world. It would be wonderful if I thought that way, but I'm not that good.

Kazuo's identity is based in hard work and ever increasing job responsibilities, much like Paul. It also rests in shedding a previous expectation, that he would be a father. To aid in forging his new married-without-children identity, he rejects the personality changes parents' undergo and denies that he ever wanted to be like that.

Most men, however, don't forge a new identity when they choose not to have kids because having kids aren't as big a part of their identity as kids are for women. Certainly, Western industrial society expects men to become fathers, but it's a weak, muted, nonurgent kind of expectation. It's the norm but not the powerful norm of becoming a mother.

Don't get me wrong. The men weren't resistant to change. They simply wanted to be in control of the changes, they wanted to choose the changes, they didn't want the changes dictated by the needs of a child.

Chapter 11

Mixed Feelings

> To summarize, it is not surprising that the majority of not-mothers I spoke with are challenged by moments or periods of internal questioning related to their childless state, no matter how committed they were to that state. Participants experienced rumblings and engaged in speculations about what might have been if they had had children. Rumblings were not considered problematic by most, but rather just temporary musings that happen from time to time depending on circumstances. . . .
> Weak moments were most often associated with a mild emotional tone, like wistfulness, or a feeling of generalized anxiety about the future. Only occasionally were such rumblings described as painful. (Carolyn Morell, 1994, pp. 108-109)

Morell's childfree women experienced rumblings at the death or illness of a family member, during transition times, times when work was stale, times when they were going through a period of boredom or loneliness. Sometimes rumblings happened at family gatherings when children were present. To see how men compared with women on this issue, I asked the men if they had any regrets or felt a sense of loss for having not had kids. This chapter contains everything they said in response to that question. The majority, in contrast to women, denied that they had any regrets or sense of loss.

WHAT IF? REGRETS

Some men occasionally wondered what it would have been like if they'd had a child. How would life today be different? Jerry, the single, Jewish newspaper artist, wondered what it would have been like if he and Betsy, the woman with whom he had all the compatibility problems, had gotten married.

I came close to being a parent, for the sake of this woman. She is now married and she's quite thrilled with having a child. It's a slightly weird experience for me because I can see this child who's now 2 years old, and I think, "What if? This could have been mine under different circumstances," which is strange, because I don't have that much interest in kids.

I feel a loss of normalcy. I'm different from the norm because I'm 42 years old, I'm not married, and I'm the only person in my department who doesn't have kids. So I'm not an average, normal American citizen. My disinterest in having kids has had a major impact on dating and relationships. I already have a problem because I'm short, because a lot of women want tall men. Then, for me to come out and say, I don't want kids, drastically cuts down the number of women I can date. During the last round of dating I met a woman I liked very much, there was that chemistry, but she was divorced and had two kids. I was really attracted to this woman, but I had to put on the brakes because it was a package deal. That's happened with a number of very nice women. I've had to back off.

I also have a certain amount of guilt from my religion. Judaism, like most organized religions, has the mandate, "Thou shalt multiply and have children." Continue the species. I have some discomfort because Judaism was so devastated by the Holocaust that there are messages from certain quarters that say, "You now have an obligation to have children, maybe have a lot of them, because so much of our religious population has been massacred."

Greg, the deputy head of a primary school, likes children and calls his charges "my children." Both he and his wife Judith are around children all day so I hardly expected him to have any regrets, yet he said:

We have a village fair and you see families and you think, "Maybe." It's not a very strong pull, but you realize that a lot of activities revolve around families, and you think, "What am I missing here?" That's one occasion that I feel it. Or when I read the village magazine and it's all, "We'd like to congratulate the Smiths because their son has just gone off to university, or the Joneses whose daughter has just got married." That's where I feel the loss.

Bob, the utilities engineer who suffers from depressive episodes, said both he and his wife enjoyed watching friends' and relatives' children grow up.

I'm sure that if it's your child, it's an even more wonderful feeling. I see the freedom I've got from not having children, but I'm also aware of the joys that they can bring. I sometimes think how neat it would be to watch an infant become aware of the world and develop language and experiment to find out things. From an intellectual point of view it would be fun to watch children grow. On the other hand, I like to go sailing and I don't think, "Gee, it would be neat to teach my kid how to sail." If there were a scale from one to ten as far as missing anything, it would be around one most of the time with an occasional peak at a three over some poignant moment. I don't feel, "God, I blew it." Instead I feel, "God, I wish I'd learned to sail earlier."

LEGACY REGRETS

How did these men feel about not leaving a legacy to their own flesh and blood? Men for centuries have acquired material goods precisely because of how proud they are about being able to bequeath fortunes to their heirs. Roger, the wood products salesman whose colleagues tease him when ill-behaved children enter the display room, experiences some of that regret.

I don't have any heirs. That is unfortunate. I often wonder what will happen to all my earthly goods when I'm finally gone. Who should get those? I don't know the answer to that question. Will I give everything to some foundation somewhere? I don't know.

If I were to say I've never had a moment's regret about not having children, I'd be lying. There are times when it would be nice to have a kid doing something worthwhile with his life. A young fellow came in yesterday, one of my clients, one of the best contractors I know, a gentleman and a scholar. He came in with his son, who is 2 years old and a perfect, adorable little boy. I have a molding rack with samples, and he went over to the molding rack and he picked out these samples, and he's as happy as if he had sense. His dad and I conducted our business, then he told the kid, "Now we have to go. I want you to put the molding back, and you may have one piece." The kid puts it back where it goes and holds up one piece to dad. Dad tells him, "You may have that piece." The kid says, "Thank you." Dad says, "Say goodbye to Roger," and the kid gives me one of those little waves. At times it would be nice to have a kid like that.

But I didn't and I can't and I won't. The tradeoff was there. I didn't have a wonderful, well-behaved, cute little kid, but I also won't have all the problems my client will have. In life you make choices, and it's a choice I would make again.

Paul, the electronics engineer who's now a vice-president of his company with seventy people under him, said that while his pragmatic side can see the potential benefit of children and while he wouldn't be thrilled to be a parent, he could adapt.

One area that does cause me pause is a selfish thing, who's going to take care of me when I'm old and decrepit? It's something I gotta think about. But, the way I live my life is, if there's a big gray issue that I don't have an answer for, I shelve it. I know eventually I'll either come up with an answer or an answer will present itself.

When I talk to someone my age who has done the parent thing, I discover that because of the children, they haven't done much except raise their child. They haven't climbed mountains, kayaked wilderness rivers, backpacked in the desert, experienced people from different cultures, gone to school for 9 years and had a great time doing it. In an egotistical manner I have a sense of loss in that there is a lot of knowledge that I've gained that will go to waste because I'm not passing it on to anyone, not letting someone learn from my mistakes. In that selfish manner there is that connectivity to family that I'm not going to have, because I'm not even close to my nieces and nephews.

THE FAMILY NAME

Male college students were given a list of reasons why men might take on fatherhood and asked what's most important. They said the main thing children provide fathers with is love and emotional satisfaction, second, children carry on the family name and bloodline, and third, children are fun (Mackey, 1996). So it came as something of a surprise that only a small minority of men regretted not passing on their name. One was Murray, the CAD designer with the pampered rescued dog, who also regretted good friends drifting away after their children were born.

The one big issue is the family name. I'm the one who's going to end it, unless my sister wants to change her name back to her maiden name. I'm the only male in the family left. I had a boss once who said, "If you don't have children, who's going to pass on your soul, your religious soul?" I said, "Well, I'm not religious, so that's not an issue with me." Then he said, "Who's going to pass on your name?" I said, "It won't get passed on. I'm going to end it. After all, whole families die in car accidents, so, so what?"

Another man concerned about his name was Ben, the rural library clerk, who inherited his father's impatience with children.

The biggest thing I'm missing for not having kids is observing the curiosity of a child growing up, learning and seeing and experimenting with things. It would be wonderful to provide them with experiences, take them to the lake, take them to a planetarium show, and see how they develop.
What bothers me occasionally is the genealogy line—my grandparents, my Dad, me, and the family name stops right here. I could have continued this on. Which is what life is all about, it's a continuation. Everything ends right here because of my decision. Every so often that thought crosses my mind. But so what? In my wife's family their name has ended because they had all girls who took their husbands' names.

Steve, the airplane painter with the coffee executive wife, told his parents as soon as he'd had his vasectomy.

I didn't want them to expect grandchildren when they're not going to come. I got a blank stare from both of them. Deep shock. I was the last one to carry on the family name. My family settled in the Appalachians in the 1700s. There's actually a national monument, a museum, in Tennessee dedicated to one of my ancestors. But the family tree never really got bushy. My father was the last one. So my parents were hurt.

Anna and Arnold Silverman (1971) say the family name is an issue for men because they want to leave behind some physical evidence of their existence. "Fatherhood often offers a way of fulfilling this need. If a man can have a child, or, more accurately, a son to whom he can pass on the family name, he feels he has achieved a degree of immortality" (p. 94).

CHRISTIAN CROSS EXAMINATION

Colin, a London university computer center manager, says his regret is the attitude of religious people.

Our department secretary is a Christian and I regret to say she has very fundamentalist views, which are totally opposed to mine. She tells me it's not natural to not have children. "Why do you not want any children?" "It's not what I want to do with my life." "But it's natural to have children." "Ahh, no it isn't. It's a choice." Where fundamentalism is concerned, they abdicate the right to choose. Where the argument comes up, people don't want to exercise their right to choose, so they duck out of it. "I can't choose this because there's an ideology I have to follow." When fundamentalists meet me, there's a bell in their heads which says immediately, "Abnormal, abnormal." It's tiresome, but pointless to argue with these people, it's like shouting in the wind.

Daniel, the piano teacher who takes muddy bike rides when he gets depressed, had similar views.

There's a problem when I *don't* know where other people are coming from when they ask me why, and, the other problem is, when I *do* know, especially people very into Christian family values. If you want to stay on good terms, because you work with these people, and you've got 10 minutes to get your lunch down and get on to your next class, you're treading on very thin ice. Discussing my decision, in inoffensive but clear and direct terms, when I know their belief is that God has ordained marriage for the rearing of children, has to be handled delicately. It's an intimate, complex issue that takes a long time to make sense of to others, and conservative Christians won't talk about it at an appropriate level.

Howard, the last man to be introduced in this book, is a 38-year-old electrical goods retail manager and has worked for the same company since he was 17. He and Georgina, his wife of 12 years and a hospital ward manager, live in a London suburb. Because Georgina has been dead set against having children since she was a little girl—never had any maternal instinct, she says—the decision to remain childfree was agreed before they married.

Howard is a dedicated trouble-shooter for his company. He travels 60,000 miles a year, likes stores in difficulty, likes solving their problems in about 6 months time, and moving on to the next. He has tackled the problems of 30 stores in his 21 years for the same company. What he values most is being able to come and go as he pleases when he is not at work. He has several cars, does all the maintenance work on them, and does all the do-it-yourself work on the houses they have lived in. When we did the interview, he was going to spend the weekend refurbishing the kitchen and then he and Georgina were taking off for a fortnight's holiday in Ireland, driving where the spirit moved them.

Howard, too, regrets that he is queried by fundamentalists and says they use innuendos having to do with his virility.

People often think the reason we don't have children is because we can't. They say, "You say you decided not to have kids, but aren't you covering up a medical problem? Yours doesn't work." That attitude is especially strong in Asian men who want boys to carry on the tradition and the family. So if a childfree man is unsure about his decision, then that yours-doesn't-work attitude can be disturbing. Personally, I don't feel any need to argue or prove the point.

PARTNER REGRETS

Who has the harder time finding a partner? Graham, model decision-maker and salesman intent on early retirement, said, absolutely, it is men. "If you're a single man and you meet prospective mates and you say, 'I don't want children,' that has undertones of irresponsibility. A woman says, 'Oh, he just wants to piddle about and have affairs and be a bit of a tosser. I want a man who's going to provide and be fun and be a friend. I've finished messing now and I want a sensible relationship that's going to be good for me and my career, and yes, my children.' Single men who don't want children are viewed with suspicion."

Doug, a 47-year-old community activitist and stress avoider ever since he left the Air Force:

My decision not to have children has been a two-edged sword. I live a very low-stress lifestyle and I have a lot of financial freedom. I've never had to worry about other people, it's just been me. The downside is, it has really restricted my opportunities for partners because most women want children.

It's getting better now because women in their forties are at an age where they already had them and they're out of the house, or they decided they're not going to have them. I wasn't going to marry someone and then announce, "Oh, by the way, I don't want children." There are at least a half dozen women I could have married along the way had I wanted children.

The single men, with the exception of Arnie, who works in computers where all the women say they aren't going to have children, agree with Graham. That makes the biggest regret expressed here—the trials and tribulations of finding a partner.

Which begs the issue. Until we recall Chapter 6, "Avoiding Mistakes." If a man says he couldn't possibly have been disappointed with his children, he isn't about to go on and on about regrets. Regret means you've done something that wasn't very smart. Consistent with the denial of disappointment is the denial of loss. It is a contradiction in terms to seek out men who have mixed feelings about their voluntarily childless state. If they were ambivalent to the point of thinking they'd made a mistake, they'd correct it. They'd have a child.

Chapter 12

Men and Overpopulation

After three decades of global fretting about a population explosion, about a world with too many mouths to feed running short of basic resources, it looks as if the "demographic transition" is spreading rapidly around the globe.

Some poor, densely populated nations with high growth rates such as Pakistan and Egypt seem headed for disaster. It is hard to see how they can supply twice as many people with the basics of food and fresh water.

World wide, however, the number of people being added to global population is falling with each passing year. The UN's Population Division believes that the highest global growth rates are behind us and we will never see their like again. This is our gift to the future (Nicholas Schoon, 1998, p. 15).

THE MISSING MOTIVE

When I had finished discussing personal motives with each of the men, I asked, "Do you feel there were any reasons missing?" Half the men said, "No, I don't think so." Then I pointed out that I had intentionally omitted overpopulation concerns. Everyone said, "Ahh," and expressed some degree of worry, but the level of their concern varied greatly. The overwhelming majority said they had chosen to be childless for private reasons and if they had wanted children, by God, they would have had their two. Only six chose to be childfree principally because of the global threat.

It remains to be seen how women and men differ. Sharon Houseknecht (1987) found 32% of American women gave fears of population growth as a motive to remain childless compared to 14% of

American childfree men. On the other hand, in Britain not a single one of Jane Bartlett's childfree women gave overpopulation as a factor in her decision. Only decent survey research can settle the actual percentages. I'll start with the comments of the men who took the threat least seriously.

POPULATION CONCERN A SECONDARY REASON

Dale, 41-year-old retired Jaguar mechanic, discovered zero population literature at 15.

It's not my primary, number one reason for choosing not to have kids. But even a teenager can realize that we have a population growing at such an exponential rate that it's going to overtake us. In 30 years we're supposed to be up to 30 billion. Right now it's hard enough to sustain 6 billion. Back then I thought, I don't really want kids, but if anyone asks me, I can give them these good external reasons not to. I'm not an eco-freak. If I had a mad desire to have a kid, I'd go ahead and do it. But the idea behind zero population growth is so obvious. It mathematically makes sense, the numbers behind it.

Jerry, the newspaper artist, said it was something that arrived later in life as a bolster for his earlier decision.

I've got a strong environmental sense which has increased over the years. Not having kids started out as a personal lifestyle choice, but it makes it easier to justify because the impact of too many people in the world is so severe. Too many people out there have kids because it's expected, although most guys are basically indifferent.

In a great amount of the world having kids is still a sign of macho and virility. Even in America in some minority populations the way you prove you're a man is you get somebody pregnant. Obviously a child is a physical, tangible sign that you're virile. In some populations around the world, you've got to have kids because you need farmhands. Or it's religious, "Thou shalt multiply," or cultural, "Don't let your enemies have more kids than you. Outbreed them, get a numerical advantage." Population control seems to be fashionable only among the more educated, Western industrialized nations. There's a lot of the world where the environmental message isn't getting through. Others who should be heeding it aren't listening.

Frank, a systems analyst and marathoner from Manchester, England, said that Great Britain is overpopulated but it's largely ignored by most people.

It's at the root of social problems in schools, long-waiting lists at hospitals, roads overcrowded, greenbelt disappearing. There should be more positive incentives for managing families and numbers of children to keep the population stable. The population issue should be a part of everyone's decision today to have children. A lot of people have children to replace themselves, or carry on the family name. I meet somebody new at work and they say, "You married?" "Yeah." "Have kids?" "No, no kids." Then there is this gap and they go on and talk about something else. They don't usually ask why, but you get this incredulous look of, "You're married and you're not having children?" It's the thing you're supposed to do if you're married. It pulls the carpet out from under parents to come across others who are content and well-rounded without children.

I asked Ted, the meditating instrument repair technician, if overpopulation and environmental concerns played any role in his decision to have a vasectomy at age 26. They hadn't, the vasectomy was strictly for personal reasons.

But I see overpopulation as the number one problem in the world. It should be part of any decision about having kids now. I look at my friends and so many who don't have the money are having another child. They're raising peons. Even in America if you don't have the means to educate a child well, it's a crapshoot. These kids are not going to get the education, the opportunities, they're going to end up at the lower end of the socioeconomic spectrum and the cycle will continue.

Bob, a utilities engineer who likes to take his little sailboat out alone, had this to say:

I started being concerned about population growth when I was quite young. I've got pessimistic about it. I expect some fairly mass extinction of people from one of these new viruses. You could have a virus with a 2-year incubation spread through the air, and you could have it all over the world before anyone had symptoms and we knew it was there. That happens all the time with other animal populations. I don't see us acting rationally enough to prevent it.

I am very much for controlled population. It's gotta happen, sooner or later, so why not sooner? Maximizing population never seemed like a reasonable objective for the human race. When it comes down to me, though, while it would have kept me from having a *large* family, I'm entitled to my two. I've always had this fear of some kind of big disaster. It used to be nuclear war. Why would I want to bring a child into the aftermath of a nuclear war? Now it's some type of ecological disaster. Frankly, when I think about not having children, I see that as one of the benefits. I don't have to worry about that anymore.

Paul, the company vice-president for whom five acres in the country is no longer enough land, said:

Just over my short lifespan I've seen the increase of urban sprawl, the tax issue of supporting schools, a host of sociological reasons. But my personal reasons are on equal footing with the environmental issue.

As a biologist I have learned about the carrying capacity of the land, how many of a species can exist on a particular type of environment, how connected all those very different species are to each other for the survival of the whole, and clearly we have disturbed that in a giant sense. So far the environment has adapted. We see coyotes living in inner-city L.A., peregrine falcons nesting in downtown Manhattan. But we're also seeing the emergence of bacteria and viruses that are resistant to all of our best stuff. There's going to be a point at which the balance is going to tip. Unfortunately, the more children we place on the planet, the quicker that's going to happen. I don't think that we can reverse the trend.

It's Mother Nature's revenge. We're going to get what we deserve. It will be ugly, so I don't want to be around for it. On the other hand, the hopeful part of me says that the planet has taken a lot of abuse already and continues to be resilient.

Simon, the Buddhist inner-city music teacher, said:

For me it was a secondary reason. We're by nature selfish. When I look around at my family and close friends, they want children, so they're going to have them. Arguments about overpopulation don't make any difference. Nor do rational, personal arguments. I wish I could get more out of my friends about their attitudes toward having children, but I rarely can. Basically they want 'em, that's usually what it comes down to.

OVERPOPULATION A PRIMARY REASON

Steve, who paints airplanes and plans to climb Mt. Everest, started off his interview with deep disappointment that he hadn't had an opportunity to express his concerns about overpopulation.

The world is overpopulated and if we want to make a difference, it would be to not reproduce. That's how I'm making the world a better place. There are too many cars on the road, and we're using up resources rather than maintaining them.

I first got concerned in my twenties. I read the literature of Zero Population Growth and I thought, why is this material such a big secret? I'm a rational, methodical problem solver and it hit me in the face. All the problems in the world that you see on the news and all the proposed solutions, why is nobody saying, maybe if we had less people? If a couple has two children, with longer life expectancy, the population is still going to expand. When the social security system was written into law, people weren't expected to live past 64. Now people are living to 74 and the system can't handle it. As life expectancy gets longer, the rules must change.

Ben, a country library clerk whose close relationship with his spouse was a primary motive for not having children, also spontaneously brought up overpopulation.

Both of us are environmentalists concerned about the dangers the increasing population poses for the future. I think that so many problems like crime and traffic are due to the overpopulation. We have to stabilize the population. It was a consideration 20 years ago when I had my vasectomy, even then. If we don't have any children, that helps out a little bit. It also will help if I can blend my environmental concerns with my art. I always wanted to be a wilderness photographer. Never quite made that, but my etchings and my prisma colors can be concerned with the juxtaposition of things, like beautiful mountains with a packed city at the base of it, smokestacks and traffic. It gets me the way people can't stand to see undeveloped land. To me, no, we need the space to breathe. We've got to fight the trend to cut it down, pave it over, and build more houses.

"I recently read Al Gore's book, *Earth in the Balance*," said Thomas, a hotel sales and marketing director.

It's a damned good book. It got the wheels turning like, "Wow, this is a serious issue." I got to looking at all the things in my life that are affected by overpopulation. The fact that I can't mountain bike on trails because urban sprawl has wiped out the trails. There's no longer a sense of community because people live so close to one another they bicker and fight, the not-in-my-backyard syndrome. Oh, god, traffic is a major problem. Then there are only so many resources to be divided up among the population.

When I have a problem, I look at the worst case scenario: What do I need to do to prepare myself for it? Once I'm ready for that, man, anything less is just great. So I see this problem of overpopulation and I'm pessimistic about it because it's such a bad situation. Therefore I'm not going to have children to help me solve this problem.

Nigel, a computer programmer whose childfree choice has serious consequences when it comes to dating, said:

I became aware when I was about 14 of the amount of damage that's being done to the environment by human beings. I thought, if I have to argue in favor of the population being reduced, which is what has to happen, I must be consistent in my life with that position. I must also change my lifestyle in terms of consumption, if we're going to achieve an ecologically sustainable society, where on balance you construct as much as you destruct the environment. We are so far removed from that, that it's going to take generations for us to ever reach that state, even assuming that as a society that was what we decided to do. Most people are not prepared to make any changes in lifestyle and the long-term trends are going in the opposite direction. Toward advertising agencies creating false demands for products instead of promoting engaging in activities. Taking a class in martial arts is not going to spoil the environment the way buying a new car does. Toward McDonalds and Burger King instead of restaurants selling organic food. We're light years away from that.

"Taipei was the moment that convinced me not to have children," said Alan, an elementary school librarian.

It's overcrowded, filthy, dirty, throngs of people, traffic jams. Human beings may have wonderful potential but we're wrecking it by having way too many. Why would I make a baby? Shelly [Alan's wife] recently read that if human beings vanished from the face of the earth, only two other species, not counting domestic pets, would also vanish. But if ants disappeared from the face of the earth, hundreds of other species would also vanish. Human beings are insignificant, except that we're overwhelming the planet. If we could get human population under control, there's no reason why every human being in the world couldn't have the U.S. standard of living. At current population levels it's not possible. Taipei is a horrible place. I lived in the suburbs with rice paddies on one side, but this abhorrent conglomeration of human activity on the other.

In my lifetime human beings are not going to wreck the earth, but I have no hope that human population will be voluntarily controlled. There are European countries now that are encouraging their citizens to make babies because they're concerned about labor shortages. As long as surplus labor is a part of profit-making for huge corporations, we're going to have surplus labor on this planet. There are powerful human beings who have a strong interest in continued population growth. I used to support the Sierra Club, Friends of the Earth, dozens of environmental groups, I was writing checks all the time to every group you could imagine. I've stopped, because it's hopeless. Now my philosophy is MAPing. Maintain, avoid, protect. Maintain our lifestyle without harming the earth. Avoid what we see happening around us. And work to protect it.

My focus, tentatively, for the rest of my life is going to be the Greater Yellowstone, the largest wild place in the contiguous United States. National Park designation? That's a temporary designation. We were in Costa Rica and in the national parks peasants come in, cut down the forest, plant crops and graze animals. Costa Rica doesn't have the resources to push them out, and if they did, where would they push them to? If a warden goes in and says, "You can't do this," the warden would be killed. These are desperately hungry people. Look at the poaching that happens in the African wildlife refuges, trying to protect the last black rhinos on earth. But hey, black rhino horn sells for $200 a pound and people who are watching their children die of starvation, they're not going to go in and kill the rhinos? Of course they are. Even in our Southwest, farmers are saying, "Yes, I know the law says I'm only allowed to run my pumps one day a week, but if I see my crops dying, I'm going to turn on my pumps. And to hell with the people down river."

Walter is a lecturer in computer technology in nursing who dislikes children as much as *Star Trek*'s Captain Pickard:

The global population issue influenced my earliest thoughts on having children. One of the first political books I read was Paul Ehrlich's *The Population Bomb*. I was a member of the Young Liberals in the early to mid-seventies and they were concerned with that issue, and I've held on to it until today. I'll use an analogy to why my wife is a vegetarian. The main influence on her decision to become a vegetarian is the fact that you can feed a lot more people in the world on a vegetarian diet than you can on a meat-eating diet. She felt she couldn't be part of the meat industry and all the ramifications of that in relation to people in developing countries. Because so many resources go to grow cattle and other meat products in the developed world, the developing countries are missing out on essential food products. My early reasons for not wanting children were that there are plenty of children in the world anyway. And plenty of people who do want children. Fine. I don't, and part of it is that a child born into a Western industrialized country uses up a lot more resources than a child in a less developed country. For several years my wife and I've adopted a child by proxy. We donate £15 a month to Action Aid to sponsor a child in Kenya.

REALISM, NOT IDEALISM

Even though many of these men subscribe to zero population growth ideology, that's not why they chose to be childfree. They made their decisions for personal not political reasons.

Those reasons hark back to social and economic realities. It is becoming ever more difficult to be a father today. The responsibilities of rearing children have grown enormously. Fathers are now expected to be both breadwinner and childcare provider. Fathers who divorce may end up supporting, financially and emotionally, two families. Fathers are threatened today by rapid and ruthless economic and employment change that undermines their ability to care for dependents. Men don't deny the above reality for *other men*, their brothers, uncle Bob, and the man next door. So why is it so difficult to say these realities are equally possible for oneself and that to have a child could end in bitter disappointment?

I reread Paul Ehrlich's *The Population Bomb* (1975 revised) looking for any mention that voluntary childlessness was one of his proposed solutions. Back in 1975 all he said was that we shouldn't have more than two, and he urged people to quit pressing friends and relations to have children. In his more recent book, *The Population Explosion* (1990), he suggests that *some people not having any children* could make a difference.

A reasonable goal for the United States for the next decade or two might be typical family sizes of one or two children, averaging 1.5, only a little less than the 1.9 we have now. With no change in family size (and a small reduction in immigration), the Census Bureau projects that our population will stop growing and start shrinking gradually around 2040, when there will be over 300 million of us. But if more Americans take the responsible step of having no children or only one, we could much sooner end growth, with a smaller peak population, and begin slow shrinkage. At the same time, we could reduce the chances that our children would face a draconian Chinese-style population-control program if and when the U.S. government awakens to the need. (p. 228)

Root Cartwright, head of BON, says the overpopulation issue is the ultimate rebuttal to people who accuse the childfree of irresponsibility.

Because you can say back, "Well, actually the population of the world is going to increase by X million by the year Y and where are we going to put them all? So by my not having kids, I'm making room for yours." The way some people argue against you, if you can't get them to simply respect that it is your right to make this choice, you can then bring in this issue that is completely distinct from the personal sphere. Overpopulation is the human race's greatest failure, that is, to acknowledge and deal with it in time. There is no value in numbers once you get up to the numbers we've got. Ever increasing numbers means a worsening quality of life for every individual.

Chapter 13

The Father Connection

It is very hard for women to avoid thinking about a new baby, but it is quite easy for men to do so. . . . The male parent does seem to be at quite a disadvantage. He is probably less attached to his newborn infant, and socially unprepared for the role. In good enough circumstances a young woman will have the help of her own mother in starting to care for a new baby, but what support is there for a young man? Does his father come along and show him how fathering can be done? And what would this actually mean? One can imagine very easily the newly promoted paternal grandfather finding every reason not to be too involved with his son. Maybe he has a busy job that he cannot leave—and what would his employers say if he asked for grandpaternal leave?

This is a very familiar model of fatherhood, which many men in the grandfatherly generation know well enough—absence. Absence from the birth itself, absence from the nursery, and later from the school, and so on. It is only in the last twenty years or so that it has seemed right to question such a role. (Sebastian Kraemer, 1997, pp. 93-94)

Absence. Distance. Disinterest. Abuse. Leslie Lafayette (1995) says childfree men more than women cite abuse as their motive for remaining childless. "Logic, or perhaps a less emotional approach to the issue, serves some men well in this area. They have seen the devastating results of abuse firsthand and know what it can do to a child. They do not try to fool themselves into believing that it won't happen with them, that somehow they will do better" (p. 150). But before we get to dads, what did the men have to say about their moms?

MOM'S INFLUENCE

No man described his mother as abusive and only two hinted theirs' were neglectful—Simon, the inner-city music teacher, and Bob, the utilities engineer who felt abandoned by his dad. Mother seems to have little to do in a negative way with a man's decision not to have children. In fact, several moms were still pushing for their sons to have a child. In contrast, not unexpectedly, "Virtually every woman I interviewed attributed her decision in large part to her relationship with her mother," Jeanne Safer (1996) has said. "Whether their bonds with their daughters were terrible or terrific—and frequently they were an all-too-human combination of both—these mothers shaped their daughters' destinies and made a major contribution to their selecting a radically different way of living" (1996, p. 94). Safer also says it was common for women who had traumatic experiences with their mothers to be early articulators.

I wondered if it was this direct for men and their fathers. I asked them: Did your dad enjoy being a father? What kind of a father was he? Is your decision connected to your relationship with him? Did you want to be different from your dad?

THREE TYPES OF FATHERS

The men's fathers could be sorted into three types: good, disinterested, and abusive. Half the men said their father had influenced their decision, half said he had not. The sons of good fathers said Dad had *not* influenced them, the sons of the disinterested dads were divided, some said yes, some said no, whereas all seven sons of the abusive dads were unanimous that their fathers had determined their choice, exactly what has been found among early articulating women whose moms were abusive.

Let's take a look at these dads, starting with the good guys.

GOOD FATHERS

Thirteen of the men's fathers were thought of as good fathers. Colin, who would rather have taken cooking than metalwork, says his dad bequeathed to him his wanderlust and taught him at age 8 the whole of the London underground. Jerry, the newspaper artist, says his hardworking father accepted his decision not to have children, that he is very close to both parents, and that he wants to move back to L.A. to be near them.

University nursing lecturer Walter says his relationship with his father wasn't close but that his father kept an eye on what his children were up to. Paul, the company vice-president, says he was raised in an Ozzie and Harriet family and that his parents, celebrating their 50th anniversary, were great. And Microsoft Gordon is proud that he and his dad are a lot alike, both computer programmers not given to talking about emotional stuff.

Michael, the psychology professor, says his father was a dear, wonderful man whom he mistreated as an adolescent, but emulated by also placing value on higher education. "I am a chip off the old block," says Alan, the elementary school librarian. His dad profoundly influenced his attitude toward marriage and business ethics.

If his father had been an influence on Bill, the trekking sports medicine therapist, it would have been *towards* having children. They were close and Bill remembers him fondly. Both Japanese Kazuo and Iranian Nathan left me with an impression of a conventional, traditional upbringing in which conscientious fathers fulfilled their role as providers. Doug, the community activist, says his parents were great, but stressed him out with their emphasis on school. Howard, the retail troubleshooter, is another chip off the old block, and proud of it.

Steve, the airplane painter, described his overly conscientious father like this:

> My father had been a naval officer and he ran a tight ship. He made it very clear what he expected. And he inspected what he expected. My father never spared the belt when we were children. Sometimes I chose the belt, and he delivered. He wasn't at all religious, but we went to church every Sunday because everybody that he worked with went to our church. So it was a see-and-be-seen attendance thing. He never talked to me, like, "When you grow up and have children of your own." He never put it to me like that. So I wasn't driven away from parenthood by my father.
>
> On the other hand, I was aware in my teens that I was bringing financial burdens on my parents that they didn't anticipate. You know, wreck the car, things like that. My actions hurt them financially and made me feel guilty. If you have children, who knows what mischief they're going to get into and you're going to be financially responsible for? How do you plan for that? It was hard enough paying for college for the three of us. My mother was a teacher and my father was a plant manager of a small paper mill.
>
> Sylvia [Steve's wife] had a talk with my dad the last time they visited and she told him that we wanted to be in control over what happened in our lives. She said it seemed like there was this formula that you grow up, get married, have children, and it's mindless. My father said, "That's what we did." So maybe if he'd thought about it, he'd have done it differently.

DISINTERESTED FATHERS

Ten of the men's fathers were basically uninterested in their children. Ben, the rural librarian, says his mother brought up him and his sister, and that his dad just hung about in the background.

Frank, the marathoning systems analyst, says he might as well have grown up in a one-parent family.

Murray, the CAD designer, says he had an in-the-background dad and so did all the guys in his ratpack. "We kids just existed, there was no affection there." For Thomas, the Portland hotel sales manager, his parents' divorce was a major life event and he ended up taking care of his younger sisters. Bob, the utilities engineer prone to depression, thinks that he might not have been a good father—too distant and cold—like his dad.

Hugh, the freelance violinist, also had a disinterested father, a telephone engineer. "He wasn't the sort of parent to go off to school matches and shout support. As far as my music, he suffered it. When I practiced, he used to go down the garden and saw wood."

Dale, the Jaguar mechanic and early retiree, had a dad who was not only disinterested, but physically distant.

My parents got divorced and he left when I was 11. I saw him a few times until I was 17 and then I didn't see him for 15 years. Right before he died I saw him twice. Kids and grandkids never came up. We never talked much about anything that mattered. Never.

Arnie, from Swaziland, says his dad distanced himself from his children by packing them off to boarding school at age 7 and calling them home only on the occasional holiday. Greg, the deputy head of a primary school, had a dad who also distanced himself by often being away on business.

My father was the traditional businessman away two or three nights a week and very often we wouldn't see him from Monday to Friday. He was a man a lot of people had a great deal of respect for. That's something from his character that I would like to have. But he was away a lot, he worked hard. My mother always said that we had to share him. When I was young, it didn't really bother me. But over the years, I would have liked to have had more time with him. He died at the age of 66, and I particularly missed him the 4 years after he died. I'd look for him to tell him something and say, "Oh, I can't find him, he's not here anymore." Before that, when he was home, he'd commute into London every day, and I used to go on that same commuter train to Dulwich to my school and I'd look around at these gray, gray men and they were old at 25, 30. They had that haunted look of, "We have to do this daily grind up to London." I knew I had to do something different.

Daniel, the piano teacher and gardener, had another classic disinterested dad.

My dad was introspective, a gifted artist in the broadest sense of the word. I had a very bad relationship with him from the age of 8 to 18. My father is not the best of communicators. In times of crisis he can be brilliant.

But generally speaking he keeps himself to himself. He is someone who definitely needs his privacy, his space, and his quiet. He brought a very big family up in a very small space because he insisted on living where all his friends were. The point is, he created this situation, it was a kind of crazy rebellion against his childhood once he got married with kids. He brought us up in squalor, and then, naturally, had a great need to get away from it.

ABUSIVE FATHERS

Seven dads were downright abusive. You've read how sales manager Roger's father had a cruel streak, and that Roger never wanted to do that to a child. You've read how music teacher Simon's father was an extremely frustrated and angry man, verbally and physically, who hit his children quite regularly. Ted, who repairs musical instruments for a living, was the emotional dump for everything that went wrong in his dad's life and has ceased communication with him. Phil, the geography teacher, said his impoverished childhood included a violent father who you'll read more about shortly. The other three abusive fathers belong to Nigel, Graham, and Matthew. Here is what they said, starting with Nigel, the 32-year-old computer programmer.

My father was a very strict disciplinarian, but that didn't seem to work with my sisters. My mother was a martyr, she might protest, but then insist on suffering anyway. I did feel she was on my side, while my father wasn't. My mother was a blamer and I felt unfairly blamed a lot, but she did the best she could.

My dad was hoping we would be fantastic children, academically brilliant, without his having to help us. He had the belief that you should learn to do things by yourself. There were times when he did try to help me with my education, but he wasn't very good at explaining things, or seeing things from my point of view. He had a siege mentality as far as raising children was concerned—you have to force your children to be good and do well. He was an intimidating guy, very disturbing. There were only a few occasions that he beat me, but I was very scared of him.

My mother wasn't happy about my decision not to have children because it made her feel that she had been a failure as a mother. My father typically reacted, "Nonsense, you *will* get married and you *will* have children," and I thought, "Well, you can tell me that, but there's nothing you can do about it." There was desperation in what he said and he was trying, again, to intimidate me. I didn't talk to him at all for a number of years.

Now, while I dislike him at one level, I can be sociable to him at another level. He said he'd help me when I tried to buy a flat, but he didn't offer to help me when I was unemployed. He said he'd pay my bills until he saw how much they were, and then he backed off.

I can hardly believe I'm related to him. The only way he shows any connection to me is financial. For my birthday he gives me £50 or £100, which to me is a lot of money.

I would have expected Graham, the 32-year-old salesman, to confide in his physician father about his vasectomy, but he said that other issues needed to be cleared up first.

I lived with my father after my parents split up. He was two parents rolled into one, and then some. He made a lot of sacrifices bringing me up, which is not to put him on a pedestal because he was a bastard at times. He was under a lot of pressure and could overreact. I saw him doing everything, working, cooking, it was very wearing for him. But if you say, I want a child, then you should be prepared to make whatever financial, emotional, and timely sacrifices are required.

The talk he had with me, warning that childraising is a difficult task, I think he did because he'd seen me do a number of things with which he strongly disagreed, and he thought the next dumb thing I'd do was have children. I used to be concerned that he didn't have faith in me as an adult capable of making my own decisions, I no longer think that, but we have a communication problem as a legacy from those days. We've never had a pint-of-beer-down-the-pub relationship. He is the Big I Am. He's a very successful, intelligent man, a hard act to follow. But when he was bad, he was very, very bad. I would like to be closer to him than I am. But it requires that a specific set of circumstances and conversations take place between us, and I've got to get to that stage of maturity for us to have them, because I've got to be fair to him. I could tell him about the vasectomy and he might have a reasonable reaction, but he might not, and until we've crossed those emotional bridges, it's not worth risking. It might alienate us so that the conversations we need to have, the bridge-building, would become harder.

Matthew, the geriatric nurse who works out regularly with his punchbag, said he was from a textbook dysfunctional family.

I was beaten up by my father, and my mother was a battered wife. I know what it's like to be hit as a child. I know what it did to me. My dad's a very dominant man, powerful man. He worked hard as a wagon driver, he's a big, physically strong man, and he had complete control over us. I remember getting beaten up with a cricket bat for stealing from Woolworth's, and a couple of weeks later, my backside was black and blue, and we went into a shop and he stole a doll, in front of me, for one of my sister's Christmas. What a hypocrite. He didn't have it to be a father. He didn't have the time. He had his own problems, his debts, his drink. Eventually abused children grow up and tell their parents what they've done and when they realize it, the parents have got the rest of their lives to live with regrets. My father still puts my sisters down. My wife can't understand how I've come out of that family.

At the age of 14 I wanted to die and I took an overdose because I'd done something wrong, I don't remember what, but my parents and brothers and sisters went out to the zoo. As a punishment I had to stay by myself. I remember thinking, "If this is life, then I want to die." My mother said they had forgot something, come back and found me, otherwise I would have been dead.

Phil, a part-time geography teacher, also had a father, a coal miner, who beat his children and wife.

He was occasionally extremely violent, when he drank a lot. He could be very responsible, when he was sober, but my father is a negative influence for having children or imagining happy families. My mother was a positive influence. Even though she was unhappy, she had a very responsible attitude toward us even though we were neglected by him. As a young man I was very bitter about my father's cruelty. It took me until my late twenties to understand why he was the man he was. The nature of his work was horrible. He did a rotten, dangerous job and hadn't a great deal to show for it. He felt frustrated because he was intelligent and he knew what was going on, but he couldn't do anything about it. Also his father had beaten him, and he might talk about what a bastard his father was, but the style then was not to talk about *yourself* at all. No communication of feeling or personal reflection. He wouldn't express any weakness at all. Any kind of emotional display was seen as weakness and that was the last thing he did.

DADS' AND SONS' DECISIONS

When men have good dads, good role models, fathers' questionable behaviors (which, by definition, are rare) have no connection to what kind of decision maker they were. Looking at the decision types of the men with good dads, there were even numbers of early articulators, postponers, and acquiescers. Looking at the sons of disinterested dads, there are six early articulators, two postponers, and two acquiescers. Then looking at the sons of abusive fathers, five were early articulators, two postponers, and *none were acquiescers*.

We have a small hint here of a relationship between abusive fathers and early articulators, which Jeanne Safer has reported for women and their mothers. Remember, though, that only half the men saw their dads as influential, so a man's relationship with his father apparently is not as instrumental in his decision as a woman's relationship to her mother is.

Another family factor that put the men off having children were crowded, cramped living conditions. There were complaints from eldest sons of always having younger sibs in tow, or of the logistics of six people sleeping on a 19-foot boat during holidays. Living in grandmother's house packed with aunties and uncles was compared to Chinese water torture. And certainly large families were part of the frustration experienced by several Catholic fathers who abused their sons.

We must also consider that *men who become parents may have a similar kind of distribution of good, disinterested, and abusive fathers as men who don't become parents.* Scott Coltrane (1996) found in interviews with American fathers that their dads had been relatively uninvolved in family life. "Most of the men reported that their fathers were 'not really there' when they were growing up. Many said they lacked a true connection or sense of intimacy with their father, even though they feared, respected, and sometimes played with him. Feeling dissatisfied with their own fathers in various ways, many of these new fathers vowed that they would 'do it differently' "(p. 121).

The problems absent fathers bequeath their sons are at the heart of Robert Bly's (1991) *Iron John*. Bly says that in men's gatherings since the early 1980s, he hears over and over, "There is not enough father." He says he has begun to think of his own father not as someone who deprived him of attention and companionship, but as someone who himself had been deprived, by his father, mother, and culture.

A SOLUTION TO DISINTEREST

What can we do about the lack of participation by fathers in their children's lives? It would certainly help if family planning associations and services cared as much about men as they do about women. A woman is "pregnant," but what do you call the man involved in that pregnancy? There isn't even a term for him. And shouldn't he be party to discussions about what to do with that pregnancy? Shouldn't someone at least find out if he's ready for fatherhood?

"If we could be indicted for neglect, we would be indicted for neglecting the role of men in reproduction and sexuality," asserted Jane Johnson, vice president of affiliate services for Planned Parenthood Federation of America. . . . "We never give young men much of an opportunity to contemplate their right to choose whether or not to parent; it is imposed on them." In conversations with young men across the country, Johnson learned that most would not be pleased if their girlfriend became pregnant because they were not ready for parenthood. (Edwards, 1994, p. 78)

Chapter 14

To Sum Up

Most men have the concept of responsibility drilled into them from the time they are very young. . . . "What kind of world is this to bring a kid into?" is a question that never had more relevance than today. I believe that a man is more likely to ask such a question, and here's why: men have a more cynical view of the world around them. . . . The concept of parenthood is a sobering one for mature and thoughtful men, and they are deeply concerned about the responsibilities incumbent in such a decision. Furthermore, they have few illusions about the world around them. (Leslie Lafayette, 1995, pp. 151-152)

Fertility rates are falling around the globe, the threat of overpopulation is lessening. The clearest correlate of the decline in birth rates everywhere is the education of women. Closer to home, one in five American and British women is deciding to have no children at all. Again, it is associated with greater education. Many of these women are part of a couple, so more couples are deciding not to have children. Just how many more we don't know, because fertility data are not collected on couples, only on women until very recently, when the first data on men were collected.

What role are men playing in the fall in birth rates? What are the men like who make the choice not to have a child? The thirty men I interviewed provide a glimpse of what that man is like.

THE CHILDFREE MAN

The typical childfree man does not want dependents. He doesn't want children, he doesn't want to manage people. He doesn't have that many people in his life because he wants as simple a life as possible.

His work is very important to him and he enjoys what he's doing. He isn't a high flyer, isn't working to get rich, and has to be able to change jobs if his interests shift. He's a lifelong learner and wants time for further education and travel. He is an aficionado of adult activities. He is drawn to artistic expression and likes making things with his hands.

He wants to keep the stress in his life to a minimum, and having a quiet home and agreeable partner are ways to relieve stress. Making a relationship work is important to him and he puts as much time into it as does his partner, who tends to be as independent-minded as he. Another way he reduces stress is through long-range planning, particularly financial planning.

He is concerned about global overpopulation. He figures that if some people shouldn't have a child at all, and he have never felt the need, why not let it be him? His father may or may not have influenced his decision. If Dad was disinterested, distant, or abusive, he is more likely to have a son who has no interest in raising children.

He denies he has regrets over his decision not to procreate, only that it can make finding a partner of like mind difficult. He also denies that he could have been disappointed with his children, had he chosen to have them.

What more can we say about him? Here are the answers to the questions we set out to explore in Chapter 1.

PATERNAL RESPONSIBILITY? NO WAY

The men talked to me with the same heightened sense of responsibility that childfree women express. They said that if you have children, they are your life's first priority and you'd better do it right. If you reckon it is impossible to get it right, conditions in society being what they are, then the responsible thing is, don't do it.

Notice how their ideas about paternal responsibility were less personal and more societal than women's. It wasn't so much that the needs of a child would overwhelm *them*, quite the contrary. The problem was that they as fathers couldn't prevent children from falling prey to a host of unhealthy pressures from society. Historian Laurie Lisle (1996) has said of nonfathers: "Liberal or idealistic men who believe in gender equality or co-parenting are sometimes more reluctant to undertake fatherhood than traditional males who feel no obligation to share child care. Opting for childlessness often seems more honorable to many of them than taking on halfhearted or irresponsible fatherhood" (p. 160). So the answer to the question, "Is responsibility a big issue for men" is yes.

NO BIG DEAL DECIDING

For women it's a major life decision, everyone agrees, because having children is more important to women than men; children are women's *raison d'etre*. Jeanne Safer says childfree women's decision-making process is problematic, complex, inconclusive, ongoing, unfolding, and traumatic—an identity crisis from which they must "forge an alternative feminine identity" to give life meaning. Carolyn Morell (1994) concurs: "Women who remain childless must forge and live out an alternative path" (p. 144). The question here might be, "Was there any sign that *some* men agonize the same way women do and must forge a whole new identity when they aren't fathers?"

The answer is no, except for Kazuo from Japan. Whether they were early articulators, postponers, or acquiescers, the men hadn't lost any sleep over it. Either they were never interested in having children, or they never felt a need to be a parent, or the woman they were interested in didn't want children. Graham is the only man I've met who went through any kind of lengthy, rational process.

Most studies of childfree couples find that women more than men are the initiators of the choice. One study found that nearly half of a group of childfree married men said that if their spouses decided they wanted children, they would change their minds. None of the wives said they would do so (Houseknecht, 1987). On the other hand, a Washington D.C. survey found among parents that 38% of the men versus 11% of the women said they had had children because their spouse wanted them (Dalphonse, 1997).

These findings might explain why more men than women are acquiescers. To explain why more men than women may be early articulators we need to look to the proportions of the sexes who dislike kids. Perhaps it's more culturally acceptable for men than women to express a dislike of children, but the fact is, 43% of childless men gave this as a motive versus 26% of women (Houseknecht, 1987). Here, over half of the men did not like children.

In conclusion, the *importance* of the childfree decision is very different for men and women, and so too is the *process*. Future surveys may well find a greater proportion of acquiescers and a smaller proportion of postponers among men than women. It also will be interesting some day to compare the proportions of early articulators, postponers, and acquiescers among fathers and childfree men. How many fathers will say they knew as little boys that they really wanted to be daddies? How many fathers postponed deciding, but did an internal debate of the pros and cons and decided independently that they wanted a child? How many acquiesced and made no real decision at all?

I WOULD HAVE WONDERFUL KIDS

A big sex difference has to with doubts about one's adequacy as a parent. It's a major motive among women but apparently not among men. A small minority of the men I interviewed said they could have been disappointed in their childrearing. The majority view was that if they had chosen to have kids they would have been wonderful fathers and their kids would have turned out great. Houseknecht (1987) reports that not one study previously has asked this question of men. Perhaps men's denial of parental inadequacy lies in the powerful messages boys receive growing up: "Be the best you can," "Be superman," "Never say you can't," and "Never admit mistakes" (Harris, 1995).

How deep does this denial run? What would the younger men have said if I'd asked, "What would have happened if you had gone into another occupation for which you lack the talent, skills, training, and interest? Could you possibly be disappointed in your performance? Even if you'd given it 150%, could you have been a successful brain surgeon? Rocket scientist? Professional football player?"

I think they would have protested the comparison. I don't think most men, even childfree men, see fatherhood as an occupation that requires talent, skills, training, and deep-down interest. To the younger men, any man, if he gives fathering 150%, he won't be disappointed with his performance. Only the older men see that they might not have been successful.

MY DAD WAS INDIFFERENT

If we are to believe the books about childfree women, almost universally they say their mothers contributed to their decision. Here only half the dads were said to have influenced the men, but there was a hint that father abuse led to being an early articulator, which also has been found in childfree women and their mothers. The major way dads influenced their sons was through their indifference about being a father. Sons' disinterest mirrored their fathers', but at a point in history where if you aren't interested in doing something, why do it? Unlike the women and their mothers, they certainly did not think their fathers had made too many sacrifices, given too much and got too little in return. The lack of emotional ties between the men and their fathers was striking and poignant.

NO HASSLES HERE

The men all agreed that women get more pressure from all directions—society, families, workmates, men, other women, the media. Doug, the community activist committed to a stress-free life, said:

They're almost railroaded into thinking that's what they have to do in life, there are no other options. Little girls are given dolls and encouraged to play house, which gives them a strong mindset of what they're going to do when they grow up, and men don't have that. It's something men don't think about, so when a child is on the way, it's kinda like, "Okay, I guess I'll try this out." Men allow themselves to get into this without thinking through the consequences.

Most men are competent in their jobs, but outside their jobs, they're amateurs, struggling along, they haven't thought through the big questions in life, and they're doing major things that they didn't consider beforehand. Children are one of the big ones in terms of personal impact. Most guys grow up thinking, "I'm going to get a nice job, a nice car, a nice apartment, I'll go on nice vacations, I won't have money problems." All this is out the window once they have kids. Sit down with a bunch of teenage guys and say, "Tell me about your life 10 years from now," and they'll talk about a cabin in the woods, a sailboat, or owning an airplane, but you won't hear much about kids. It's just not in their consciousness.

When these men were challenged, interestingly, it was by women colleagues, in addition to Mom. The men didn't talk of feeling pressured by advertising, the media, and social institutions. They didn't feel discriminated against at work, the only complaint being that parents were free to leave for events such as kids' soccer practice, and they had no comparable excuse. Indeed, the reactions of male friends and colleagues were mostly supportive: Fine. Good. If that's your decision, stick to it. Other men didn't care.

The only two men who are seriously challenged are from Japan and Iran. They, literally, cannot go home again because of prejudice by everyone against their childfree state.

When I asked about losses and regrets, not many had much to say, beyond how hard it was to find a partner. The women's literature is full of accounts of being treated like you have a disease—you're seen as deviant, neurotic, selfish, disturbed. Either the men are into denial big-time, or society in general has become more tolerant and men are reaping the benefits of this greater tolerance far more than women.

CONTROL? NOTHING TO DO WITH ME

Women easily say one reason I didn't have kids was to keep control of my life. The men didn't like the word "control." The portrait painted earlier of the childfree man is a man who wants to be in control of his life, but this isn't how he wants to phrase it. I asked Root Cartwright, head of BON, to explain.

Having a handle on everything is incongruent with valuing freedom and independence, which you've said they all preferred to talk about. Control conflicts with how many men like to see themselves. They like to think that they can throw a change of socks into a holdall and jump on a plane and do whatever they want to do. The guy who sits at his desk for 40 years and collects his gold watch and drops dead isn't something that men aspire to anymore. So there aren't many men today who write a business plan for their lives, like Michael Heseltine (Conservative politician) who, when he was at university, wrote on the back of an envelope *when* he was going to enter Parliament, *when* he was going to enter the cabinet, and *when* he was going to be prime minister. Men today would not regard that as a worthwhile exercise.

VASECTOMY? I'LL GET AROUND TO IT

Why so few vasectomies? Several mentioned squeamishness regarding medical treatment, which is typical of men. Second, if men go to a doctor about the procedure, they're going to be asked—why do you want to do this? How certain are you? Are you married? How does she feel about it? Uncomfortable talk on a taboo topic.

Third, men see contraception as a woman's responsibility, so it's up to her to implement the decision. A fourth possibility: Men have less commitment to the decision, whatever their motives are. They want to leave their options open, "just in case."

A fifth explanation came from Root Cartwright. He says too many men equate a vasectomy with no longer being macho, virile, a real man.

I can think of five friends who have had their quota of kids, they're all great parents, and I'd bet that none of them has had a vasectomy, even though none of them intends to have any more children. It is almost impossible to talk to them about it. There's this confused idea that you're going to be unmanned. That your sexual function is going to be impaired. These are very common misconceptions tied up with old-fashioned ideas about masculinity. People used to equate the ability to father children with the size of your dick or your sexual athleticism, and they similarly equated vasectomy with castration. Although all the literature says a vasectomy doesn't change a thing. In fact, sex is better because you're more relaxed, free of the anxiety of an unwanted pregnancy.

But if you do something that you are encouraged to think of as irreversible, you're gambling on the fact that you're not going to change your mind and that your circumstances aren't going to change. That's a big step to take for a young man. What puzzles me more are men my age (47) who are in relationships that look set for the long haul, they have their couple of kids, why they don't is a much greater puzzle, because their wives aren't going to be on the pill after 30 odd years. It's gotta be this culturally inspired fear that it's not going to work properly afterwards.

I also asked Root why more men aren't speaking out about their voluntary childlessness.

Men don't like drawing attention to themselves. A childfree couple I know did an interview for one of the tabloids. They are highly respectable, high-flying bankers in the City and the day it appeared, by the time they got to work, the little oik in the mailroom had photocopied this piece and pinned it up all over the building. Obviously, people don't want that kind of attention drawn to themselves. In some employment situations attracting notoriety to yourself is bad news as far as your employers are concerned. Imagine if you've got a line manager above you who is a devout Catholic. He won't keep his religion out of his professional life, and on a personal level, men don't like to be conspicuous. There's also the fear in some men that they're going to be thought wimpy or gay or they can't get it up, if they talk about being childfree.

THE FUTURE OF VOLUNTARY CHILDLESSNESS

Voluntary childlessness will continue to increase in the United States and United Kingdom. Major factors will be the continued rise in higher education and full-time employment among women. As the pool of postponing women who eventually decide not to have a child expands so too will the number of male acquiescers. But it is also possible that basically acquiescing men will change into postponers who decide on their own to control the mounting stresses in their lives by foregoing fatherhood.

They know that women's expectations of them are to be both breadwinner and caregiver. They know how much time it takes to be a good dad. They know how a disinterested dad can ruin a childhood, not to mention drugs, gangs, and juvenile delinquency. Looking beyond personal motives, they see the adverse effects of global overpopulation all around them. The rate of growth may be slowing, but it isn't slowing fast enough to halt the deterioration of our public infrastructure, exploding urbanization, and worrying resource depletion.

In a study of men in New York City, Kathleen Gerson (1993) found a third of them had no interest in being breadwinners or caregivers. "As divorce, postponed marriage, and permanent singlehood have become more common, so has the tendency for men to postpone becoming a father, to eschew fatherhood altogether, or to lose contact with their children. Although studies of men's childbearing patterns are rare, it appears that men, like women, are more likely to postpone parenthood or to remain childless than were their counterparts three to four decades ago" (p. 6).

Gerson concluded, "A growing proportion of men now find parental ties, like marriage itself, voluntary and discretionary. Fatherhood as an economic, social, and emotional institution is increasingly based on what men want and find meaningful rather than on what they are constrained—by women and social regulations—to do" (p. 273).

In the United States, men clearly want the choice of how many children they have to remain their prerogative. Men don't want the government telling them how many kids they can have: That's for them to decide. Men don't want the personal to become political, with the result that U.S. politicians won't touch population growth issues with a ten-foot pole. Family size is not only a taboo topic in state legislatures, it isn't discussed anywhere—in the media, arts, churches, not even over the back fence (Pryne, 1998, p. A24).

"Over the back fence" discussion keeps the topic in the personal arena and it's as good a place to start as any. Just lean over and lend your neighbor this book.

Appendix

REASONS WHY PEOPLE SAY NO TO KIDS

Check as many of the reasons below that apply to you. Then review the sets of reasons and select the three sets with which you most identify. Put their letters here:_____ _____ _____. With which set did you LEAST identify?_____

Set C Reasons
[ ] You have plans for the future that you definitely want to carry out.
[ ] Your personal, long-term security would be threatened by the financial responsibilities of children.
[ ] You feel children's needs come first and when you're a parent, you don't have as much control over your life.

Set D Reasons
[ ] You see how disappointed many parents are with their children and prefer to avoid that.
[ ] You doubt that you'd be good "parent material."
[ ] You want to avoid having to deal with children in the event of divorce.

Set E Reasons
[ ] You want to devote lots of time to your career and/or community work.
[ ] You want the freedom to change jobs.
[ ] You want your employment situation free of financial obligations to children.

Set F Reasons
[ ] You want the freedom to come and go as you please.
[ ] You love to travel and want to go whenever you choose.
[ ] You want to avoid the routines children impose and enjoy new experiences.

Set I Reasons
[ ] You have never felt any particular need to have children.
[ ] You identify with not having to be grown up and serious all the time.
[ ] You're happy as you are.

Set M Reasons
[ ] You don't want to spend your money raising and educating children.
[ ] You don't want dependents, job insecurity being what it is.
[ ] You have serious doubts about the high cost of raising a child to 18.

Set N Reasons
[ ] You really don't enjoy children all that much.
[ ] You do not want the responsibilities of raising a child.
[ ] You aren't really attracted to child-centered activities.

Set O Reasons
[ ] You believe that by not having a child, you are not contributing to overpopulation.
[ ] You believe that the world's resources are diminishing too rapidly to sustain any quality of life much longer.
[ ] You prefer to enjoy other people's kids than have one of your own.

Set R Reasons
[ ] Your relationship with your partner is too good to jeopardize by having a child.
[ ] You don't want your partner's primary role to be that of a mother or father.
[ ] You think your partner might not enjoy being a parent.

Set S Reasons
[ ] You do not have the patience to raise kids.
[ ] You find children wearing and stressful after a few hours.
[ ] You do not have enough energy for children.

Set T Reasons
[ ] You want time and space for yourself.
[ ] You want lots of time for personal development and further education.
[ ] You do not want to give up the time you now spend on your interests and recreation.

What do these set letters stand for? The motives represented in the statements, namely, C for control; D for (avoiding) disappointment; E for employment; F for freedom; I for identity; M for money; N for not attracted to children; O for overpopulation; R for relationship; S for (avoiding) stress; T for time. A popular set of three motives among the men interviewed was T-F-I. What were your strongest reasons?

References

Apodaca, Patrice. (1998, June 15). On their own terms. *Seattle Times*, Section E, p. 2.

Bachu, Amara. (1996). *Fertility of American men*. Washington, D.C.: Fertility Statistics Branch, Population Division, U.S. Bureau of the Census.

Bachu, Amara. (1997). *Fertility of American women: June 1995 (Update)*. Washington, D.C.: Current Population Reports, U.S. Bureau of the Census.

Bartlett, Jane. (1994). *Will you be mother? Women who choose to say no.* London: Virago.

Bly, Robert. (1991). *Iron John: A book about men.* Shaftesbury, Dorset: Element Books.

Campbell, Elaine. (1985). *The childless marriage: An exploratory study of couples who do not want children.* London: Tavistock.

Casey, Terri. (1998). *Pride and joy: The lives and passions of women without children.* Hillsboro, OR: Beyond Words Publishing.

Cohen, David. (1996, September 27). Which hat shall I wear today? *Independent* Section Two, pp.2-3.

Coltrane, Scott. (1996). *Family man: Fatherhood, housework, and gender equity.* New York: Oxford University Press.

Dalphonse, Sherri. (1997 February). To have or have not? *Washingtonian, 32,* 51-53, 89-93.

Edwards, Sharon R. (1994). The role of men in contraceptive decision-making: Current knowledge and future implications. *Family Planning Perspectives, 26,* 77-82.

Ehrlich, Paul R., & Ehrlich, Anne H. (1990). *The population explosion.* New York: Simon & Schuster.

Gerson, Kathleen. (1993). *No man's land: Men's changing commitments to family and work.* New York: Basic Books.

Greenstein, Ben. (1993). *The fragile male.* London: Boxtree.

Harris, Ian M. (1995). *Messages men hear: Constructing masculinities.* London: Taylor & Francis.

Houseknecht, Sharon K. (1987). Voluntary childlessness. In Marvin B. Sussman & Suzanne K. Steinmetz, (Eds.), *Handbook of marriage and the family.* New York: Plenum Press (pp.369-395).

Kraemer, Sebastian. (1997). The fragility of fatherhood. In Geoff Dench (Ed.), *Rewriting the sexual contract.* London: Institute of Community Studies (pp.89-102).

Kupers, Terry A. (1993). *Revisioning men's lives: Gender, intimacy, and power.* New York: Guilford Press.

Lafayette, Leslie. (1995). *Why don't you have kids? Living a full life without parenthood.* New York: Kensington.

Legal & General Assurance Society. (1996 September). *Value of a mum.* London: Author.

Lisle, Laurie. (1996). *Without child: Challenging the stigma of childlessness.* New York: Ballantine Books.

Mackey, Wade C. (1996). *The American father: Biocultural and developmental aspects.* New York: Plenum Press.

May, Elaine Tyler. (1995). *Barren in the promised land: Childless Americans and the pursuit of happiness.* New York: Basic Books.

Morell, Carolyn M. (1994). *Unwomanly conduct: The challenges of intentional childlessness.* New York: Routledge.

Pryne, Eric. (1998, September 20). It's a hot potato lawmakers won't touch: Limiting family size. *Seattle Times,* p. A24.

Safer, Jeanne. (1996). *Beyond motherhood: Choosing a life without children.* New York: Pocket Books.

Schoon, Nicholas. (1998, February 2). Why the end of the population explosion is nigh. *Independent,* p.15.

Silverman, Anna, & Silverman, Arnold. (1971). *The case against having children.* New York: David McKay.

Veevers, J. E. (1980). *Childless by choice.* Toronto: Butterworths.

Waitley, Denis. (1995). *Empires of the mind.* New York: Morrow.

Weiss, Robert S. (1990). *Staying the course: The emotional and social lives of men who do well at work.* New York: Free Press.

Witkin-Lanoil, Georgia. (1986). *The male stress syndrome.* New York: Newmarket Press.

Index

Abusive fathers, 125-27
Acquiescers, 4, 8-10, 31, 52-53, 102
Apodaca, Patrice, 75
Aversion to children as motive. *See* Not liking kids as motive
Avoiding disappointment as motive. *See* Disappointment as motive
Avoiding mistakes as motive, 55-66
Avoiding responsibilities of parenthood as motive, 38, 53, 64, 130
Avoiding stress as motive, 7, 9, 20, 27, 30, 39, 52, 54, 85-96, 130

Bachu, Amara, 1-2
Bartlett, Jane, 45, 57, 60, 114
Beyond Motherhood (Safer), 80, 97, 122, 127, 131
Bly, Robert, 128
BON (British Organisation of Non-parents), 3, 6, 47, 57,120, 133
Buddhism, 18-21, 59-60

Campbell, Elaine, 47

Cartwright, Root, 47, 57, 120, 133-34
Casey, Terri, 70
CBC (Childless by Choice), 3
Childfree man, profile, 129-30
Childless by Choice (Veevers), 3, 37, 47, 52, 65, 67
Childless decision: family of origin reactions, 26, 30, 40, 58, 78, 86, 89, 91, 102; model decision maker, 5-7; types of decision makers, 4, 7-10, 131; who initiates, 74, 131
Childlessness. *See* Voluntary childlessness
Cohen, David, 85
Colleagues' attitudes toward childfree decision, 30, 43, 76, 99
Coltrane, Scott, 127-28
Control over life as motive, 60, 71, 90, 133-34
Cost of children. *See* Money as motive

Dalphonse, Sharon, 34, 45, 131
Decision to be childless. *See* Childless decision
Demographics, 3

Denial of disappointment, 44, 49,
    56, 73, 77, 80, 103, 130
Disappointment as motive, 39,
    55-56, 58-59, 61-62, 65, 87
Disinterested fathers, 40, 52, 62,
    123-25, 132

Early articulators, 4, 7-8, 14, 16,
    38
Early retirement as motive, 39,
    64, 73, 75-83
Edwards, Sharon, 128
Egalitarianism, 27, 31, 34-35
Ehrlich, Paul, 119-20
Employment as motive, 37-46, 51,
    53

Family name regrets, 108-9
Father connection, 15, 19, 70, 89,
    93, 121-28
Fear of failure. See
    Self-confidence
Freedom, importance of as
    motive, 14, 27-28, 30-32, 37,
    40, 50, 63, 72, 88, 100
Further education as motive. See
    Personal development as
    motive

Gerson, Kathleen, 88, 135
Global population. See Population
Good fathers, 122-23
Greenstein, Ben, 57

Harris, Ian, 132
Houseknecht, Sharon, 4, 25, 69,
    113, 131
Housework, 31, 34-35, 41, 51, 69,
    95

Identity, preservation as motive,
    33, 41, 59-60, 62, 69, 79, 97-
    104

Job freedom, 2, 22, 33, 37, 43, 62,
    69, 73, 94, 101, 130
Job importance, 39, 41, 43, 51, 91,
    103, 130
Job satisfaction, 44-45

Kraemer, Sebastian, 121
Kupers, Terry, 55

Lafayette, Leslie, 2-3, 13, 46, 60,
    97, 99, 121, 129
Legacy concerns, 42, 69, 90, 107-8
Legal & General Assurance
    Society, 25
Lisle, Laurie, 130

Mackey, Wade, 108
Male fertility study, 2
Masculinity issues, 60, 110, 134
May, Elaine Tyler, 25
Mixed feelings, 34, 105-111
Money as motive, 15, 34, 45-46,
    76, 79
Morell, Carolyn, 70, 105, 131

Need to have children, 7, 14, 20,
    31
Need to succeed, 56-57
Not liking kids as motive, 67-74,
    77

Partners, difficulty finding, 17,
    90, 93, 110-11
Personal development as motive,
    13-23, 28, 92
Population: attitudes towards, 1-
    2, 104, 130; overpopulation as
    motive, 113-120; stabilization,
    1, 129
Postponers, 4-7
Pryne, Eric, 136

Reasons exercise, 3
Regrets. See Mixed feelings.
Relationships: preserving
    partnership as motive, 25-35,
    38, 48-49, 59, 90, 101
Responsibilities of parenthood.
    See Avoiding responsibilities
    of parenthood as motive
Role strain, 85-86

Safer, Jeanne, 80, 97, 122, 127,
    131
Schoon, Nicholas, 1, 113

Sex differences in the childfree, 2,
    4, 23, 25, 37, 40, 57, 60, 69-70,
    744, 80, 97, 105, 113-14, 121,
    130-135
Spouses: attitude toward childfree
    decision, 6-10, 14, 18, 26, 30,
    32, 38, 40, 49, 51, 54, 67, 70,
    72, 76, 78, 82, 102; job
    importance to, 9-10, 30, 50, 59,
    82
Stress. *See* Avoiding stress as
    motive

Time and space for self as motive,
    9, 17, 62-63
Travel as motive, 16, 19, 21,78,
    81, 95

Vasectomy, decision, 4, 8, 14, 26,
    29, 115, 134-35
Veevers, Jean, 3, 37, 47, 52, 65, 67
Voluntary childlessness: future,
    135-36; pronatalist pressures,
    2-3, 109-110, 132-33; rates,1-2

Waitley, Denis, 13
Weiss, Robert, 35, 55, 66
Why Don't You Have Kids?
    (Lafayette), 2-3, 13, 46, 60, 97,
    99, 121, 129
Witkin-Lanoil, Georgia, 96

ZPG (Zero Population Growth), 3,
    116

About the Author

PATRICIA LUNNEBORG is a former Professor of Psychology and Adjunct Professor of Women's Studies at the University of Washington. She has published more than 100 scholarly articles and is a Fellow of the American Psychological Association (Counseling Division). Since her retirement, she has written several books, including *Women Changing Work* (Bergin & Garvey, 1990) and *Abortion: A Positive Decision* (Bergin & Garvey, 1992).